VICKERS VISCOUNT

Front cover:
**Dan Air's V839 G-BGLC. The airline's Viscounts
principally operated from Lydd.**

Back cover, top:
**British Airway's V802 G-AOHS was one of 70
Viscounts originally operated by BEA.**

Back cover, bottom:
**Viscount V806 G-AOYP *Island of Jersey* is
operated by British Air Ferries.**
All photographs by Alan J.Wright

Front cover:
**Dan Air's V839 G-BGLC. The
airline's Viscounts principally
operated from Lydd.**

Back cover, top:
**British Airway's V802
G-AOHS was one of 70
Viscounts originally operated
by BEA.**

Back cover, bottom:
**Viscount V806 G-AOYP *Island
of Jersey* is operated by
British Air Ferries.**
All photographs by Alan J.Wright

Classic Civil Aircraft: 4

VICKERS VISCOUNT

ALAN J. WRIGHT

Viscount Montgomery

Bri

IAN ALLAN
Publishing

Contents

First published 1992

ISBN 0 7110 2070 1

Published by Ian Allan Ltd,
Shepperton, Surrey; and printed
by Ian Allan Printing Ltd at their
works at Coombelands in
Runnymede, England.

Abbreviations

BAF	British Air Ferries
BCal	British Caledonian Airways
BEAC	British European Airways Corporation
BMA	British Midland Airways
BOAC	British Overseas Airways Corporation
CAAC	Civil Aviation Administration of China
FAA	Federal Aviation Authority
HP	Handley Page
IT	Inclusive Tour
KLM	Royal Dutch Airlines
MoS	Ministry of Supply
SAS	Scandinavian Airlines System
SBAC	Society of British Aircraft Constructors (later Aerospace)
TAA	Trans-Australia Airlines
TCA	Trans-Canada Airlines
VC	Vickers Commercial

Previous page:
**The Viscount's classic shape retains its attractive
appearance despite its age. British Air Ferries
continues to operate the type successfully
although this particular example (G-AOYO) was
sold in 1985.** *BAF*

Above:
**British Airways continued to operate the Viscount
until the early 1980s. In this instance G-APIM is
on duty on the Scottish routes.** *AJW*

Preface

When the prototype Viscount appeared at the 1948 SBAC show at Farnborough, it aroused considerable interest amongst the industry and public alike. Nearly 45 years later any appearance at an airport still draws the attention of onlookers because the aircraft retains the qualities of a thoroughbred.

Through the years much of the credit for the Viscount's existence has been given to the wartime Brabazon Committee because of its foresight in anticipating the need for such a machine. Indeed, it was responsible for a specification outlining a short/medium range airliner amongst others, but with a capacity of only 24 passengers.

dent, which was also tailor-made to meet the airline's changing specification. This time there was a difference because the US industry had a suitable alternative on offer, resulting in the Boeing 727 winning most of the orders at the British machine's expense.

Back in the 1950s when the Viscount entered service, the advanced design effectively combined the comfort and service of the prewar days with the speed and efficiency of the new age. Its passenger appeal was enormous and was certainly unmatched by any other type. Similarly the Viscount quickly became popular with the airlines because wherever it was introduced, profits increased in sympathy with the soaring traffic figures. Even in the early 1960s when operating in direct

This particular vision was therefore somewhat blurred, but on the other hand the group continued to express its faith in turbine power when the pessimists were predicting high fuel costs leading to uneconomic operations.

British European Airways played a large part in the Viscount's success story because its collaboration with Vickers resulted in an aircraft of the right size. From the outset the Corporation strongly recommended that the proposed transport needed to be enlarged if it was to fulfil the needs of the expected travel boom. The airline was not quite so positive about the power plant, because at a fairly late stage, piston engines were still favoured. Fortunately, Vickers continued to support the Dart even when Rolls-Royce was experiencing teething problems in the early stages of development. The faith shown was certainly rewarded by impressive statistics for reliability and performance.

It is interesting to note BEA's useful contribution, because similar involvement in later years had a distinctly adverse effect upon the chances of the Tri-

competition with a modern jet such as the Boeing 707, if given the choice, many travellers preferred to fly with the propliner despite taking as much as an hour longer for a journey.

On the European and UK domestic routes, passengers could experience a smooth ride above any inclement weather for the first time. This led to the popular demonstration of a pencil standing erect upon a table without signs of movement. As an alternative there was always the 12-sided 3d piece (1p); a robust coin of the realm prone to making holes in trouser pockets. Hat racks installed were akin to those to be found in railway carriages of the day, consisting of brackets with netting strung over them along the length of the cabin. Many years later some of the aircraft operating in warmer climes also carried a half dozen ordinary electric fans bolted to the racks in order to give improved ventilation. Contrary to popular belief there was no truth in the report that they were the turboprops'

Left:
In this rearward facing shot, the overhead fish-net type hat racks can be noted as can the auxiliary ventilation fans. *BAF*

Below:
The Viscount was certainly one of the best of British. *BAF*

answer to JATO (jet-assisted take-off). But in the 1960s even the Viscount succumbed to more modern devices when television monitors were mounted on the overhead racks at the request of the Japanese domestic carrier, All Nippon. It was probably the first airliner to be provided with such in-flight irritation or entertainment; the choice of descriptive term depending on personal opinions.

When the Viscount was withdrawn from the trunk routes in favour of the jet types, its usefulness had by no means ended. It became the popular choice of the independents both for scheduled and IT charter work, with some of the destinations served being far beyond the range limits originally envisaged for the VC2 project. Space was found for more and more seats until even the shorter Series 700 managed to carry 71, almost double the original number considered reasonable. By this time a new generation of passengers had emerged, who were willing to accept the more cramped conditions as the price to pay for a cheap visit to the seaside. Nevertheless, they did begin to question the use of an aircraft with propellers, which to the ill-informed, signified antiquity.

Many Viscounts sold second-hand found themselves in South American and African countries before some of the nations had even joined the third world. Whether this had any bearing upon the fatal attraction that mountains seemed to possess is not known, but certainly an unacceptably large number of the type were drawn towards the solid piles of rock. Others were lost after becoming the innocent victims of aggression, but there was also a disturbingly large number of landing and take-off incidents.

The Viscount's structure was not intended to last indefinitely, but with regular inspection and renewal of time-expired components as specified by the manufacturer, the type has continued to operate safely. Nonetheless, by the mid-1980s many of the survivors were close to completing the 30 years life-span set by Vickers. It was the number of cabin pressurisation cycles that were responsible for the figure, so the possibility of undertaking an extension programme was investigated by British Aerospace and British Air Ferries, by then the largest Viscount operator in the world. With the agreement of the British CAA, the necessary work began on certain fuselage modifications, which, when completed, added another 15 years to the aircraft's life expectancy, or took the total permitted landings to 75,000 whichever was sooner. Naturally the number of airworthy specimens has steadily dwindled in recent years, but there is every sign that the Viscount will still be active in the 21st century.

When the type was in full production, Vickers won orders from some 60 customers worldwide, amounting to a return of £177 million for the 439 aircraft sold. Later the number of operators greatly increased as examples came on to the second-hand market, usually to play a large part in improving the carriers' financial position. Remarkably, it is now 40 years since the Viscount entered service with BEA and over 20 since one of the earliest members of the family became the first postwar civil airliner to be earmarked for preservation.

This distinction was accorded the V701 G-ALWF after it flew for the last time on 12 April 1972. Leaving its final operational base at Cardiff, the 19-year old machine followed the M4 motorway eastward towards Heathrow, where a brief stop was made before it headed off towards Liverpool. Undercover accommodation had been made available at the northwest airport so that Whisky Fox could escape the ravages of the weather as a museum exhibit. Much of the credit for all the effort needed to finalise the arrangements belongs to Paul St John Turner, who established the Viscount Preservation Trust in order to ensure the future of the type. Unfortunately, the project nearly failed after the need for generally improved airport security prevented public access to the aircraft at Liverpool. Thankfully the imminent arrival of the local scrapman was averted after the Duxford Aviation Society agreed to acquire the pioneer for permanent display at its Cambridgeshire site. Due to other priorities, the restoration process was protracted, but eventually the Viscount was completed and repainted in early BEA livery. It now stands alongside younger commercial types that have long since been grounded.

Subsequently several other examples of the Vicker's classic design have been preserved for posterity. While providing a fitting tribute to the magnificent aircraft and its creators, the atmosphere and character of a living specimen is naturally missing. Fortunately it is still possible to hear and see the type busily working at airports around the UK. Hopefully it will be a long time before the distinctive sound is silenced for ever.

Below:
It is now over 20 years since Whisky Fox was retired for preservation. *Alan J Wright (AJW)*

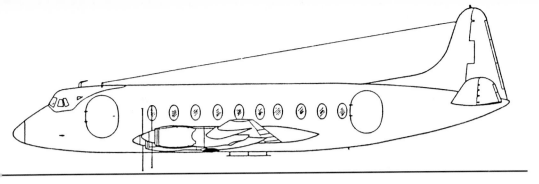

Background

Nowadays air travel is taken very much for granted for both business and leisure purposes. This was certainly not the case in prewar days when the idea of flying was not a mode of transport contemplated by the ordinary citizen. Generally it was considered something reserved for those with money who were either adventurous, foolhardy or possessed suicidal tendencies. There was undoubtedly some sense in this viewpoint because the airliners of the day were not lavishly appointed, making even relatively short sectors a test of stamina. Towards the end of the 1930s this situation at last showed signs of improvement in the UK, as more modern designs were introduced. In particular the Flamingo and Albatross from the de Havilland stable held great promise, but sadly the war brought a premature end to these types civil careers and subsequent development.

Understandably there was a greater need to produce aircraft for a more aggressive role, so for several years little thought was given to future civil requirements. Indeed, it was a period when many doubted that there would ever be a return to normality, despite promises that the army proposed to dry its laundry on Germany's Siegfried Line. When this quickly proved over-ambitious other encouragement was forthcoming, particularly for anyone near Dover where it was claimed the mystical bluebird would soon be seen. This was destined to be a little more prophetic, although most of the early sightings carried black cross markings. Of all the wartime ditties, the well-meaning warning to the rabbit fraternity probably proved the most useful, although in the event being shot was doubtless preferable to the later myxomatosis alternative. Possibly this bombardment of propaganda even inspired the authorities to consider the future with more optimism, because on 23 December 1942 the first tentative steps were taken to meet the forecast postwar demands for air transport.

Bearing in mind the extremely gloomy outlook, it was surprising that the government thought it worthwhile to produce outline specifications for airliners, but at least it helped to convince the population that all was well. On the other hand, if the worst happened at least the UK aviation industry would be in a position to supply the victors with modern equipment. Naturally, no such scheme can succeed without the creation of a committee; so it was fortunate that a few qualified people with some spare time were available. It could not have been easy to concentrate on a project not connected with the war effort, but the group, under the chairmanship of Lord Brabazon of Tara, persevered. Perhaps the task could have been made easier by employing a few redundant soothsayers, but this course of action did not prove necessary, and in any case most had heeded their own prophecies and put their crystal balls in store for the duration.

When submitted to the Government, the results of the Committee's deliberations indicated that there were four main categories in need of attention. Two involved long-haul types, another envisaged a smaller, high-speed, long range machine for mail work, while the fourth highlighted the necessity for a medium-sized airliner suitable for general use on European routes.

It certainly provided the various manufacturers with food for thought, especially since the demand for military aircraft would ultimately be drastically reduced. In 1944 a second Brabazon Committee began exploring the earlier recommendations in greater detail, with special attention paid to the operating economics of the various types of powerplants available for a 30,000lb short/medium range airliner. For identification purposes the designation Type IIA was allocated to this class, which was originally intended to become a DC-3 replacement, the first of many such attempts to emulate the success of the reliable Douglas twin. Airspeed began work

9

on a design to meet the requirements, but it soon out-grew the original Brabazon specification. At this time it was still thought necessary to provide spacious accommodation for the passengers, a standard feature in the prewar days of leisurely travel. Nevertheless, the machine was duly accepted, in due course becoming the Centaurus-powered Ambassador.

At an early stage it had been recognised that it was unrealistic to expect the new commercial aircraft to be ready for service before about 1950. Although there had been great advances made in both performance and reliability; it would take time for the postwar, rejuvenated civil aviation industry to adapt the new technology to its needs. Hence some form of interim type was necessary. In 1944 Vickers began studies of three different designs, each based on a military product and provisionally named the Warwick Continental, Windsor Empire and Wellington Continental. Since the most pressing requirement was for a short-range type to support the DC-3 on the future European and domestic routes, a civil version of the Wellington seemed to offer the best solution.

Therefore on 20 December 1944, Vickers' chief designer, Rex Pierson, presented himself before the Brabazon Committee, although the latter was not directly responsible for any short term expedients. Identified as the VC1 (Vickers Commercial 1), it was the company's answer to meet Specification 17/44. A civil version of the Merlin was originally nominated by the authorities, but Vickers had opted for the Bristol Hercules 10M which offered increased power and superior single-engine performance. Known as the series 100 in its production form, the engine had already flown 100hr in the Wellington test-bed, LN718, so it would therefore be available at an earlier date than the competitor. It was an important factor because by this time there were distinct signs that the war was nearing an end, so speed was of the essence if the new transport was to be ready for the early reintroduction of scheduled services.

Enterprisingly Pierson, the chief designer, used the occasion of his visit to discuss the VC1's eventual replacement. The Committee had already expressed its interest in the new propeller-turbine as a means of motive power for the project, considering it to offer greater promise than a pure-jet for the envisaged short-haul sectors. Accordingly the specification for the Type IIB was prepared following discussions between the Ministry and the Committee, the latter stressing the urgency for this second-generation airliner.

In the meantime every priority was given to work on the Viking, the name chosen for the VC1. It was the second use of this identity because it had previously been applied to an amphibian produced by Vickers after the first major conflict ended in 1918.

This time the bearer borrowed as many components as possible from the Wellington and Warwick in order to simplify production. Although the geodetic construction used for the military types was extremely robust; the manufacturers created a new stressed-skin fuselage for the airliner, but initially the fabric covered wing was retained. At least the risk of a foot through the floor was removed.

Any temptation to install a tricycle undercarriage was resisted despite the obvious advantages of this configuration. It would have meant some extensive redesign and restressing work on the front fuselage which would have inevitably introduced unacceptable delays. Instead, the Viking retained a tailwheel, but the mainwheel units were derived from a combination of the best features of both its bomber stablemates.

After a remarkably short time, the Viking was ready for its maiden trip aloft on 22 June 1945, which gave it the distinction of becoming the first British postwar airliner to fly. Three aircraft were used for test and development work leading to the award of a type certificate on 24 April 1946. As the first customer for the Viking, British European Airways (BEA) began to take delivery of its aircraft during the summer, enabling the first passenger service to be flown by G-AHOP on 1 September between Northolt and Copenhagen.

Once some early de-icing problems were overcome, the Viking performed well in service, on more than one occasion proving itself to be as rugged as its illustrious forebear. Since it was intended for medium range work, it was not expected to struggle above an altitude of 15,000ft or so, therefore no attempt was made to provide a pressurised cabin. Otherwise the comfort level was good in the early specimens, with adequate soundproofing, heating and ventilation. Comfortable seats were provided in the carpeted interior, each row positioned adjacent to a large square window. One less desirable feature inherited from the military designs was the formidable obstruction created by the wingspar as it passed through the fuselage. In the early days it was used to divide the two sections of the cabin, but later such partitioning went out of favour, although of course the sizeable step had to remain.

Vikings continued with BEA until 1954, having carried some three million passengers in almost 500,000 flying hours when the last specimen was retired. This was by no means the end of their careers because many moved on to serve with reputable charter companies, while others were operated by carriers of lesser means. It was not unknown for financially stretched airlines to possess only three serviceable Hercules but two aircraft. The single-engined example therefore had to await the arrival of its colleague before a swift transplant

Above:
The unpainted prototype Viking G-AGOK in August 1945. *Via AJW*

could be performed prior to departure. Truly delays for technical reasons!

Of the 163 Vikings built, undoubtedly the Model 618 was the most unusual. Built for the Ministry of Supply as G-AJPH/VX856, airframe 207 was selected to receive a pair of Rolls-Royce Nene turbojets in place of the more customary Hercules piston engines. This more potent power source was mounted in two underwing pods, necessitating some strengthening of the wing skinning, and the use of metal covering for the control surfaces in place of the traditional fabric. In addition Vickers produced a new main undercarriage for the machine, consisting of two pairs of independent legs each carrying one wheel which retracted either side of the jet efflux pipe. There was a danger that

Below:
As an interim airliner in the early postwar years, the Viking gave useful service to both BEA and the independents. This Eagle aircraft (G-AJPH) was originally powered by two Nene turbojets, but was given a more conventional powerplant in the 1950s. *AJW*

the tyres could become overheated in this position, so a protective guard was devised to remove this hazard. Once again the tailwheel was retained with the result that the runway tended to suffer from the full effect of the hot exhaust on take-off. At least it provided work for runway refurbishers following the warming of the tar.

The Nene-Viking made its maiden flight on 6 April 1948, in the process becoming the first British jet transport to take to the air. During the course of its test career, the aircraft was used for research into the problems of high-altitude, high-speed commercial operations, therefore playing a significant role in the development of postwar civil aviation. Those accustomed to the sight of the portly shape sedately droning along could hardly believe their eyes as the propellerless model streaked across the sky at an impressive speed. Even when cruising it could maintain 393mph over a range of 345 miles, a feat demonstrated on 25 July 1948 when it carried 24 passengers from London to Paris (Villacoublay) in 34min 7sec. Obviously the pilots had ignored the standard notice above the airspeed indicator which stated that 270kt should not be exceeded! These were impressive figures indeed, especially since it was only 39 years earlier that Bleriot had just managed to chug across the Channel.

After its valuable test career had ended in 1953, the aircraft was sold to Eagle Aircraft Services and

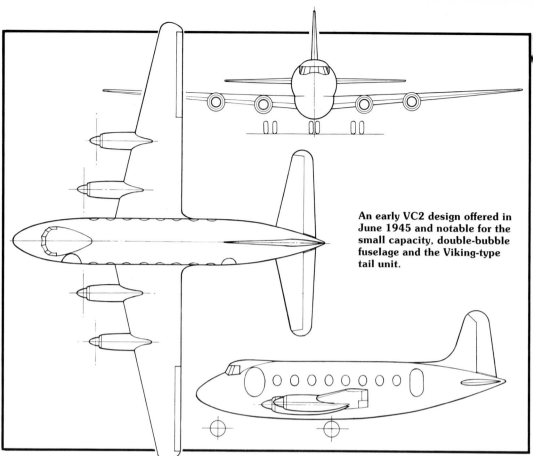

An early VC2 design offered in June 1945 and notable for the small capacity, double-bubble fuselage and the Viking-type tail unit.

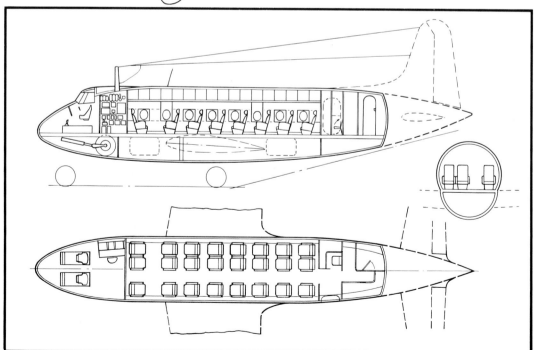

July restored to a more orthodox appearance. From 1954 it was employed for both passenger and cargo work, this time playing a part in the introduction of cheap charter flights. It all came to an end in 1961 when its expired certificate was not renewed and, after a few months of inactivity at Heathrow, the mortal remains of the pioneer met an ignominious end when dumped in a gravel pit at Bedfont, Middlesex. To its owner it was merely an ordinary Viking requiring much work to restore it to its former glory. Nowadays this would not constitute a problem however long the project, but in 1961 aircraft preservation was not a popular pastime.

Even before the first flight of the Viking in July 1945, Vickers had submitted three proposals to the Ministry for its eventual replacement. Two were similar 24-seat airliners with the option for pressurisation, while the third was slightly larger and able to accommodate 27 travellers in an unpressurised fuselage. There were so many different Government departments claiming to have an interest in the subject that it is surprising that any progress was made. Despite these built-in potential obstacles, agreement was reached in May the same year whereupon general outline descriptions of the Type IIB were issued.

Still envisaged as a 24-seat machine, the provisional study anticipated that it would be powered by four propeller-turbine engines and that pressurisation would be a requirement. Interestingly, although the flightdeck was to be designed for three crew members, even at that early date it was specified that consideration should be given to eventual two-crew operation. Performance figures expected were not unreasonable and called for a still-air range of some 900 miles after cruising at 270mph at an altitude of 10,000ft. In fact the fuel capacity to be provided was sufficient for 1,200 miles and the aircraft was to be capable of climbing to 30,000ft, a considerable advance on the heights flown by the types then in service.

One month after the Ministry's thoughts were aired, Vickers produced firm proposals for its new VC2. It easily met the Government's figures since the 24 passengers would be carried over 1,040 miles (1,674km) at 297mph while reaching an altitude of 20,000ft en route. The fuselage was to be built on a double-bubble principle, with a length of 63ft 9in (19.43m) supported by a mainplane of 88ft 0in (26.8m) span. After evaluating the available powerplants then under development, Vickers opted for the Rolls-Royce Dart which was designed to develop 1,130ehp for take-off. However, at this point in time there was no guarantee that the engine would be successful, so as an insurance against possible set-backs the company was prepared to use the Armstrong Siddeley Mamba or Napier Naiad as an alternative should the need arise.

This caution was understandable because the performance of the propeller-turbine of any type had still to be proven in the air. During 1945 Rolls-Royce modified the Derwent 2 turbojet to drive a 7ft 6in (2.29m) diameter five-blade propeller by means of reduction gearing and an extension shaft leading through the mouth of the intake. This experimental engine was known as the Trent and although it was never intended to have a future itself, its activities as a testbed proved invaluable. The Meteor 1 EE227 was considered a suitable carrier, so after the necessary modifications to the standard airframe had been completed, the combination took to the air for the first time on 20 September 1945 to mark the start of a highly successful and useful career.

In the same month as this historic event, a shuffle of the Vickers' management team resulted in Rex Pierson being elevated to the position of Chief Engineer in the Aircraft Division with group executive technical authority. His successor as chief designer was George (later Sir George) Edwards, previously the Works Manager for the Experimental Division. Undoubtedly this change brought renewed impetus to the VC2's progress and played a significant part in the type's eventual success.

Above:
It was 1986 before one of Sir George Edward's creations carried his name. The distinguished designer was honoured by British Air Ferries when one of its Viscounts (G-AOHM) was christened at Gatwick. *AJW*

Soon after his appointment, Edwards and his team carried out a detailed study of the project, paying particular attention to alternative fuselage-shapes. Following these latest investigations it was decided that a circular-section was preferable to the double-bubble design favoured hitherto, even though it would be more difficult to provide under-floor holds. Some passing attention was given to the use of a pair of Napier Double Naiads, while even a four-engined device equipped with two

13

A twin-engined version powered by Napier E128D Double Naiads was considered in mid-1946.

Darts inboard plus either two Derwents or Nenes turbojets in the outboard positions was briefly considered and swiftly rejected. But it was the Dart that was finally confirmed as the engine choice, because Edwards knew that Rolls-Royce's experience with this type of powerplant was unsurpassed. Much had been learned from the Trent and the benefits would now be passed on to the commercial model under development. In his opinion this factor and the reliability of its centrifugal compressor was sufficient to justify the faith.

Although there had been more obvious signs of action towards the end of 1945, in the year as a whole progress had been painfully slow. This fact had not escaped the Brabazon Committee's notice, so at its 61st gathering the members agreed to pass on these observations to the appropriate government department. This was no mean feat in itself, because the major upheaval brought about by the recent General Election had generated an urge for change. One of the outcomes was that the Ministry of Aircraft Production became the Ministry of Supply, so it was to the latter that the committee directed its disquiet.

Action was uncharacteristically swift because the Ministry invited four other companies to submit design studies to the Type IIB specification to guard against any possible development delays with the VC2. However, to eliminate any possible doubts about its support for the latter, on 9 March 1946 Vickers was awarded a contract by the Ministry calling for two prototype airliners. There was even a contribution of £1.8 million made towards the development and manufacturing costs. Originally it had been expected that four aircraft would be specified, so the reduction was something of a surprise. Vickers still considered that a third example was desirable so that the Naiad alternative could be assessed. This being the case, the company had little choice but to fund the construction as a private venture. Although registered as G-AJZW, the mark was never taken up, since later developments meant that the aircraft was no longer required.

On 17 April, the company formally received Specification 8/46 which laid out the precise requirements. Power was to be provided by four propeller-turbine engines, the Armstrong Siddeley Mamba being the official preference because at that time the development of this engine was making greater progress than the rival Dart. The airliner had to accommodate 24 passengers with the option to increase the total to 32 if necessary, while the cabin air differential pressure was to be 6.5lb/sq in and a maximum noise level of 60db had to be attained. Flying at a height of 20,000ft, a payload of 7,500lb (3,402kg) was expected to be conveyed 700 miles by the aircraft, which also had to have a take-off run of 3,600ft (1,097m) — even with one engine cut.

Although pressurisation was a new feature on British civil airliners, Vickers had the benefit of some wartime pioneering work on the Wellington. It was as early as 1938 that the company became involved in the subject, because it was asked to investigate the feasibility of using the twin-engined type for high-altitude bombing from a height of about 40,000ft. Bearing in mind the complex nature of the new problems constantly encountered, progress was good. Test flying of the Hercules-powered Mk V began in 1940, to be superseded by the Mk VI with two Merlin 60s a year later. However, as time passed, so the need to drop bombs from such high levels steadily receded, taking with it the official interest. Changing policy meant that the Mosquito was more than adequate for the task in hand. Nevertheless, participation in the project had rewarded Vickers with invaluable experience of pressure cabins which certainly held the company in good stead when turning its attention to the civil market.

Following the invitation to tender for the VC2 back-up contract, several designs were forthcoming including a trio of projects from Handley Page identified as the HP76, HP77 and HP78. It was the proposal from Armstrong Whitworth that was selected by the Ministry, leading to an immediate start on the production of two prototypes. Designated the AW55, the aircraft was also to be powered by four Mambas and at an early stage became known as the Apollo. First flown on 10 April 1949, the subsequent trials were successfully completed proving that the machine was more than just a second choice type. Unfortunately for Armstrong Whitworth, the VC2 justified the confidence it had been accorded, with the consequence that it attracted the orders at the expense of the rival design. Given the opportunity the latter would no doubt have proved its worth, but in reality, after some research work at Boscombe Down and Farnborough, both prototypes were broken up in the mid-1950s.

Now that there was a firm commitment it was time for a name to be bestowed upon the Vickers Type 609 as was the custom in those days. After pondering over suitable words beginning with V, the selectors finally announced that henceforth it would be known as the Viceroy. Unexpectedly it was to be short-lived. In the meantime the Government had been busily disposing of the British Empire with India one of the countries affected. Its independence in 1947 made the ruling Viceroy redundant, hardly a satisfactory situation for the namesake back in Britain. With the list of V-prefixed names reduced by one, the alternatives were reconsidered. Eventually another distinguished title was allocated which proved to be a worthy choice, for the Viscount truly belonged amongst the nobility of the land.

A more unorthodox layout using two turboprops
and a pair of turbojets was also one of the possible
projects. Not surprisingly it was quickly filed.

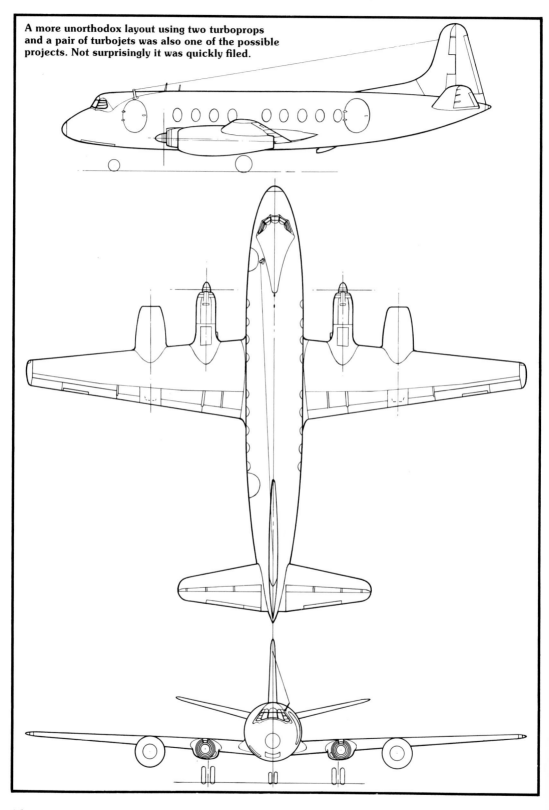

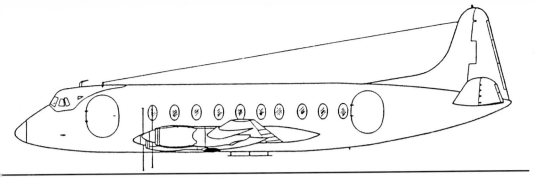

Development

The award of the development contract was certainly a welcome step forward, but it by no means ended the debate on powerplant or dimensions. Therefore when construction of the prototypes commenced in December 1946, there had been several major changes made to the original specification. Some of these were made to comply with the wishes of the British Overseas Airways Corporation (European Division) (BOAC) and its mid-1946 successor, British European Airways Corporation (BEA), because Vickers was well aware of the influence an order from the national carrier could have on future sales.

It was generally agreed that the 24-seat proposal greatly under-estimated the likely postwar demand for air transport. The prototypes therefore started off as 32-seaters which meant that the length of the fuselage was increased by 9ft (2.74m) to 74ft 6in (22.71m). When combined with the slightly greater wing span of 89ft (27.13m), the changes naturally also raised the gross weight to 38,170lb in sympathy. There was also the powerplant to consider, an important factor which was producing a note of discord amongst the interested parties. The Ministry still favoured the Mamba in view of its development programme being at a more advanced stage than the Dart, although the latter remained Vickers' preference.

However, in August 1947 the Ministry changed its mind in the light of the latest reports from Rolls-Royce, so Vickers was instructed to install its favoured engine into the second prototype, which thereupon became the Type 630. At last there appeared to be sufficient agreement to ensure a future for the Viscount, but such hopes were soon to be dashed after a series of studies were completed by BEA. These compared the operating economics when using a variety of powerplants, before coming to the conclusion that a further stretch was necessary to justify turbines. Indeed, the Corpora-

tion decided that four Merlin 22s presented the most efficient and practical solution for the VC2 in its present form.

Adding to the immediate problem was the fact that the prototype Centaurus-powered Ambassador had flown during the summer and was now undergoing its trials. It was a time when the national carrier frequently suffered from political pressure when orders for new aircraft were involved. In this case BEA was being firmly persuaded to acquire examples of the Airspeed product, which although to an advanced design, was still driven by piston engines. To further complicate the matter it was established that a similarly powered Viscount derivative would provide matching operating statistics. This fact, of course, was never proved in practice because the airline agreed to support the Ambassador by ordering 20 in December 1947. Without doubt it was a fine aircraft which enjoyed considerable customer appeal, but unfortunately its delayed service introduction did little to help its prospects.

News of the order brought a wave of gloom and despondency to Vickers, such was the seriousness of the setback. Work on the second and third machines at the manufacturer's Foxwarren hangar, located between Weybridge and Wisley, was either slowed appreciably or stopped altogether. In fact for several months there was a distinct possibility that the Viscount's career would end before it had even begun. Fortunately, there was sufficient confidence to ensure the completion of the first prototype, which was then transferred to Wisley for final assembly. By now, the Ministry was sufficiently convinced of the Dart's superiority, so there seemed little point in waiting for the leisurely completion of the second aircraft before a Rolls-Royce-powered version could be assessed. Following such observations there was only one sensible solution; install the engine in the first airframe instead. After roll-out in June registered G-AHRF, preparations were

Although the Ambassador was popular with the passengers, the type had a fairly short career with BEA. This is G-ALZZ. *AJW*

made for the maiden flight of the world's first civil transport designed from the outset to be powered by turboprops, the now generally accepted abbreviation for propeller-turbines.

The long-awaited event took place on 16 July 1948, a dreary, damp day unworthy of such an historic occasion. With the company's chief test pilot, J. (Mutt) Summers in command and accompanied by G. R. (Jock) Bryce, the aircraft left Wisley's grass strip for an uneventful 20min amble around the local area. When back on the ground the pilots both expressed their extreme satisfaction with the machine which had quickly indicated that it was a natural flier. Normally a number of snags could be expected, but a faulty fuel flow gauge produced the only item that needed attention. During the next few weeks the requisite 15hr flying was recorded to permit attendance at the September SBAC show at Farnborough.

Needless to say, the Viscount attracted considerable interest amongst the visitors, who were anxious to glean more details of this advanced new airliner. The slim lines of the engine assembly produced much comment, especially since each Dart was a completely self-contained unit offering easy access and removal. Safety measures had been considerably enhanced by the use of low volatility kerosene and crash-proof tanks in the wings, both new features at the time. In the cabin,

the passenger accommodation was divided into two sections fore and aft of the galley. Interestingly, this area still retained the time-honoured title of the stewards' pantry, although this prewar practice was already disappearing. There were 12 seats arranged in pairs either side of the central aisle in the front cabin, while the larger area in the rear possessed 20 in a similar formation. Each row was adjacent to one of the large oval-shaped windows, unquestionably the finest ever to be carried by a civil transport. As a bonus each could be used as an emergency exit. With the advent of pressurisation many thought that only small portholes would be practical, but the Viscount certainly disproved that theory. In over 40 years there is no record of a window failure being the cause of a mishap, truly a vindication of the design.

Once the Show had ended, G-AHRF immediately returned to its busy work schedule, although Vickers found the necessary time for the aircraft to visit France on 20 September. There was a good reason for this visit to Villacoubley, because it was hoped to interest a number of airline officials in the aircraft, with the prospect of some orders. As it happened, none was forthcoming on that occasion, but it was not really unexpected. Upon its return to the UK, the prototype resumed its test programme carrying military markings and the identity VX211.

18

The Viscount's windows remain unsurpassed for size and visibility and were all intended to become emergency exits if necessary. *BAF*

During the summer of 1948, Rolls-Royce was able to offer the RDa 3, an uprated version of the Dart giving a 40% increase in power over the RDa 1 flying in the V630 Viscount. It seemed an opportune moment to satisfy the wishes for an even larger version, so the designers prepared a specification for the latest variant: the V655. By increasing the size of the fuselage and wings the gross weight was raised to 45,000lb (20,412kg) compared with 38,650lb (17,532kg) reached by the V630. High-density seating then made it possible to carry between 40 and 53 passengers, while the estimated performance improvements indicated that a cruising speed of 333mph would be achieved. Although both the Ministry and BEA were keen on the idea of stretching the Viscount still further, neither considered this latest project entirely satisfactory.

Vickers promptly set about refining the specification, a task which was completed in January 1949. This time all those involved in the consultations were in agreement, but one question remained unanswered. How was the new version to be funded? It was left to the Ministry to devise some means of finding the necessary finance, but it was by no means an easy task. Jumble sales were quickly ruled out as being too slow, but then it was suddenly remembered that the second prototype was actually owned by the Government anyway. By diverting this machine into a military research programme, the resultant money transferred from another department would pay for the new stretched variant. A simple paper transaction, but one which left the way clear for one aircraft to be ordered by the Ministry of Supply on 24 February.

When Vickers had decided to abandon work on the third V609 airframe a year or so earlier, a number of its component parts had already been produced and were still stored at Foxwarren. Many

were therefore incorporated into the new V700 enabling an early start to be made on its construction. However, before this could happen they had to be moved elsewhere because the space and staff previously allocated to the project were now involved with the urgently needed Valiant prototype. As a result the latest Viscount's fuselage was built at South Marston near Swindon, while the wings took shape at another Supermarine plant at Itchen, Southampton.

Meanwhile, development flying with G-AHRF had been proceeding very satisfactorily indeed. This was confirmed on 15 September 1949 when the aircraft was issued with its Certificate of Airworthiness after completing 290 hours in the air during the course of 160 flights, all achieved in just over a year. It was the first such document to be awarded

to a turbine-powered type, so the event could rightly be regarded as a notable landmark. Nevertheless, it was not unrestricted because some important items had still to be tested on the Viscount. For instance, the pressurisation system was not completed until June and thereafter took several months of trials at various altitudes up to 30,000ft before it was fully cleared.

Similarly the summer is not necessarily the best time to test the efficiency of the de-icing arrangements, so this part of the programme had to be postponed until more appropriate conditions prevailed. In January 1950, the prototype was out-stationed at Shannon, on the bleak west coast of Ireland, for the subsequent test flying, which proved that the thermal system worked faultlessly. Four separate sorties were made in temperatures varying from 0°C to -18°C and at heights ranging from 4,500ft to 15,000ft. A number of modifications were introduced to clear several more troublesome areas such as the windscreen, propellers and around the leading edges of the Darts' air intakes, but none presented any insurmountable problems.

On 20 March the prototype entered a new phase when it departed from Northolt on its first tour of European capitals, for which it was repainted in a

The Viscount prototype was repainted in BEA's new livery prior to the inaugural passenger flights. *Via M. J. Hooks*

smart new colour scheme designed by BEA. When it returned the aircraft had flown on 70 separate occasions, covered 4,400 miles in transit and recorded a total flying time of 61hr. Previously there had been much speculation about the ability of the aircraft to fly safely on two engines thereby conserving fuel. This theory was tested by the BEA captain on board during one of the sectors between cities with no dire consequences. The technique was also employed while waiting to land at several of the busier airports, again proving it to be a practical proposition. Nevertheless, the procedure was never adopted as standard practice when the Viscount was in full service, because of the effects on the electrical system and the additional workload on the crew. During the tour virtually no daily maintenance was required on the machine, the only replacements necessary being a compass amplifier, a torch ignitor in one of the engines and the replenishment of an oleo leg.

After more routine flying throughout the spring, on 5 June G-AHRF set off for its final tropical trials

at Khartoum and Nairobi. It was expected that the aircraft would be away for about a month and was accompanied by a Valetta carrying spares and maintenance equipment for use during servicing sessions. A series of uneventful high-altitude take-offs and landings were carried out in the hot climate before the Viscount returned to its home base in July. Although Vickers' test pilot G. R. Bryce flew the V630 during these trials, the second flightdeck member was Capt R. Rymer of BEA, who assumed command of the aircraft during the various transit stages. On these sectors Mutt Summers became the second pilot with Jock Bryce relegated to the Valetta. A further 10 specialist members of Vickers' staff were present, while BEA, Rolls-Royce and the Aeroplane & Armament Experimental Establishment Boscombe Down each had two representatives on board.

Later in the month the long-awaited day dawned. At BEA's behest the authorities issued the Viscount with a C of A which fully cleared it to carry passengers. Two days later, on Saturday, 29 July

Above:
When the second Viscount prototype eventually appeared it was powered by two Rolls-Royce Tay turbojets for military research. *Via AJW*

1950, the world's first scheduled service was flown by a turboprop aircraft. The prototype actually began its temporary activities in charge of BE329(X2), departing from Northolt bound for Paris (Le Bourget) at 12.48hr at the start of its 57min journey. There were 10 special guests on board for this auspicious occasion including Peter (later Sir Peter) Masefield from BEA, Sir Frank Whittle and Vickers' Chief Designer, George Edwards. In addition the remaining 12 seats were filled by some fortunate, ordinary fare-paying passengers, who were probably wondering why there was so much fuss.

Throughout the following two weeks, the Viscount was slotted into the timetable to operate 36 return services between London and Paris, in order to supplement the Viking fleet through the busy Bank Holiday period. Total flying time was 94hr 18min and 1,516 passengers were carried, so in addition to providing some useful experience for the airline, good commercial results were recorded. Following this success, on 15 August the Viscount began a week-long series of daily visits to Edinburgh, where the Festival always created extra traffic for the London route. The journey was scheduled to take just under 1hr 45min, which was a marked improvement on the 2hr 15min allotted to the DC-3s normally in charge of the 325-mile route. After eight round trips the aircraft had flown 27hr 30min and had carried 322 passengers on what were the first domestic schedules to be operated by a turbine-powered type.

At the conclusion of its 25 days of regular airline employment, G-AHRF was returned to the manufacturer for a complete examination. Undoubtedly the opportunity to discover the customers' reaction to the new transport was invaluable for BEA, while in its turn Vickers acquired some useful practical knowledge about the aircraft's performance on active duty. Obviously confident of the outcome, the flag carrier signed a contract on 3 August for 20 Viscount 701s, the stretched version still to fly. It meant in the absence of any set-backs, it was not unreasonable to expect that deliveries of the production aircraft would commence according to plan in the autumn of 1952. If this timetable was maintained, the Corporation intended to introduce its latest possessions during the following spring, after comprehensive route-proving and training sessions.

Until the V700's first flight, all of the Viscount's development flying had been carried out by the single prototype V630, despite the Ministry's 1946 order for two aircraft. Progress on the construction of the second had been well advanced prior to the serious setback in early 1948, which was responsible for a considerable reduction in the number of man-hours allocated to the project. Originally it was intended that it would be Mamba-powered, although the wing mountings were thoughtfully designed to be compatible with the Dart. This proved advantageous when the Rolls-Royce engine overcame its earlier troubles to prove itself worthy of the aircraft, but it was already apparent that there was no longer a need for a second V630. When the Ministry used the incomplete prototype to obtain the money for the V700, the new owners decided that its military research would involve testing new systems, especially at high altitudes. To assist the airframe to reach such unaccustomed heights, it was introduced to a pair of Rolls-Royce Tay turbojets, but the combination was never envisaged as a possible jet airliner, but merely a test vehicle.

In its new guise the unique variant became the Type 663, exchanging its unused civil identity G-AHRG for the service serial VX217. The potent newcomer's first venture aloft was made from the company's airfield at Wisley on 15 March 1950, while its only public appearance was at Farnborough in the same year. Onlookers were much impressed by its short take-off run and high rate of climb, even if accompanied by noise levels uncharacteristic of a Viscount. Later the twin-jet was involved in experimental work for the Decca Navigator before it moved on to Boulton Paul for operations from Defford. From here a variety of powered control trials were flown with particular emphasis on those destined for the Valiant. Its short but useful career ended in 1958 when a hydraulic fire caused irreparable damage to the airframe. The remains lingered on until 1960 when it was finally broken up at Seighford, Staffs with only 110hr in its logbook.

At least it had a longer life span than G-AHRF, although the latter managed to amass a grand total of just over 931hr during its test flying activities. Its contribution was therefore inestimable and certainly qualified the machine for future honourable retirement in a museum. Before it became eligible to become a permanent dust-covered fixture, the V630 suffered an accident at Khartoum on 27 August 1952. As a result of a heavy landing it lost the starboard undercarriage leg, incurring damage deemed too serious for economic repair. At least the prototype was still working usefully right to the end of a career which played a major part in the air transport boom in the 1950s.

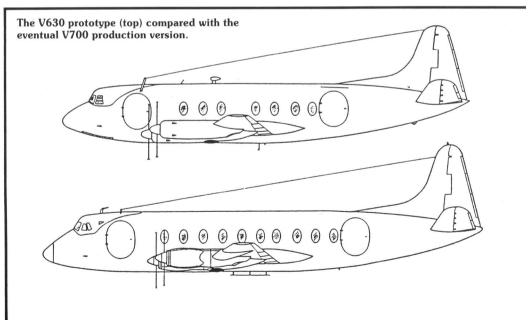

The V630 prototype (top) compared with the eventual V700 production version.

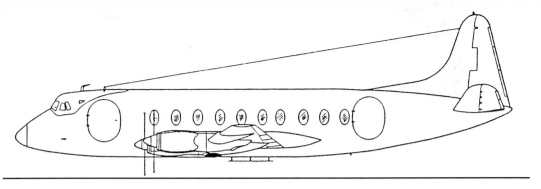

The Type 700

Once the main structure had been completed, the sections of the Type 700 were brought to Weybridge for final assembly in April 1950. The task of producing what was effectively a new design had taken only 18 months, helped to some extent by the availability of the unused V609 components. Nevertheless, there was still much work to be done if the aircraft was to make its appearance at the SBAC show in September. The next six months or so were therefore rather hectic for the staff responsible for meeting this important deadline, but to the credit of all concerned, the latest variant, registered G-AMAV, was ready for its maiden flight on 28 August. As with the first prototype, there were no major snags reported by the pilot, Jock Bryce, after

the V700 landed at Wisley in readiness for its trials. The fact that the aircraft had become the first turbine-powered type to take-off from the famous Brooklands site hardly seemed important at the time. With only a few days left in which to accumulate the qualifying number of hours stipulated by the SBAC, the Viscount was quickly back in the air to ensure that it could make its Farnborough debut.

When demonstrated in the flying display, the low-level, steep turns that were executed certainly underlined the pilot's complete confidence in the machine, giving no hint of its modest total of hours. They were certainly manoeuvres not normally associated with commercial airliners, but those were truly memorable vintage years before rules and reg-

The V700 prototype G-AMAV carried BEA's livery for its maiden flight and subsequent flight trials.
Via AJW

ulations brought an end to such performances in the interest of safety.

Compared with the prototype, the V700 had a fuselage that was stretched by 6ft 6in (1.98m) to a total length of 81ft 2in (24.77m), giving the version a much improved appearance over the rather squat V630. To compensate for the expansion, the wing span was increased to 93ft 8in (28.56m) and four of the latest, more powerful Dart RDa 3 Mk 504 engines were provided. It was noticeable that the newcomer carried a larger dorsal fillet than the first machine; since it had been found that the latter tended to yaw slightly in rough weather.

Although the aircraft was not the production version ordered by BEA, it only differed in detail from the airline's future V701 variant. Inside the cabin it could be noted that there was no partition to divide the accommodation into two separate sections. Undoubtedly the best of the 40 seats were those in the back three rows since they offered unobstructed vision through the large windows. Elsewhere the Viscount's passengers had to be content with either an expanse of wing or lengthy engine nacelle blocking the view, but this was a normal disadvantage with low-wing designs. Forward of the main cabin was the spot reserved for the galley; shortage of time preventing the installation of the unit prior to the show. The flightdeck was arranged for three crew members, with both pilots enjoying an excellent view, but generally the space allocated did not seem over-generous. On the starboard side was the rear-facing radio operator's position, so when this duty was later made redundant it improved conditions considerably.

Once the Show had ended, the V700's flight test programme began in earnest, continuing through 1952 until it was time for the tropical trials in the autumn, by which time G-AMAV had flown 250hr. On 5 October it set-off from Bournemouth (Hurn) for South Africa, flying in easy stages via Nice, Malta, El Adem, Wadi Halfa, Khartoum, Entebbe, Nairobi, Salisbury to Johannesburg, a total distance of 6,411 miles. The strenuous work accounted for 105hr of flying spread over eight weeks; the Viscount returning to the UK on 30 November. The four Darts were fitted with full water/methanol injection equipment, which proved entirely satisfactory during the take-offs from Khartoum and the high-altitude airports at Entebbe and Nairobi.

All suitable opportunities were also taken to promote the virtues of the aircraft, resulting in demonstrations at Salisbury and Johannesburg before representatives of the government, airlines and other guests. By chance 'MAV was present at Entebbe for the official opening of a new runway extension, becoming the first machine to take-off after the Governor had completed the necessary ritual. Once again, the aircraft's stay in Africa demonstrated its reliability, because neither airframe nor powerplant needed anything other than routine maintenance throughout the overseas excursion. Safely back at its UK base, the V700 prototype was prepared for its next task, namely the final series of tests required for its C of A and the completion of its de-icing trials.

Despite the extremely satisfactory progress being made, BEA's order for 20 received in August 1950 remained the only sales success for many months. There was a glimmer of hope in March 1951 when Air France indicated its intention to acquire six examples, but Vickers had to wait until later in the year before there was a firm commitment. This was received in early November when the French flag carrier signed for 12 V708s, the type number allocated to the customer by the manufacturer. Soon

afterwards it was followed by an order for four from Aer Lingus, after an earlier expression of interest in the type was confirmed in writing. Brighter prospects seemed to have dawned for the Viscount.

It is interesting to reflect that while BEA was eagerly anticipating its modern equipment, the airline was also about to modernise its DC-3 fleet. Originally 26 aircraft were earmarked for conversion by Scottish Aviation at Prestwick, but subsequently the total was increased to 38. In their new guise the aircraft were known as Pionairs, the last of which was not retired until May 1963, 10 years or so after the Viscount entered service.

After the Irish order, Vickers had to wait for another seven months or so before it was able to announce its first victory outside Europe. For some time it had been unofficially known that Trans-Australia Airlines (TAA) was a likely customer, but with negotiations still underway, no formal confirmation could be given. The airline's homeland was considered to offer ideal conditions for the operation of medium-sized turboprop airliners, with the majority of the inter-city stages well suited to the economics of the Viscount. A number of alternatives were offered to TAA, but eventually the airline specified a variant with greater fuel capacity, to enable it to fly non-stop on the longer sectors such as the 1,325 miles between Adelaide and Perth. To produce this additional range with adequate safety margins, extra wing tanks containing 230gal were fitted together with underwing attachments for optional 290gal slipper tanks. Known as the V720, the model was laid out with a two-crew flightdeck, while the passenger cabin layout could be varied between 40 and 48 seats depending upon specific service requirements.

As if to celebrate the six aircraft order from TAA, the prototype V700 was dispatched on a sales tour to India on 21 June 1952. This time 'MAV departed from Blackbushe to stage through Malta, Beirut, Bahrain and Karachi on its journey to Delhi. Demonstrations were arranged for a number of airlines in both India and Pakistan, while the air forces of both countries also expressed an interest in the type for transport purposes. On completion of its Asian wanderings, 'MAV headed off to Baghdad to enable Iraqi Airways to inspect the machine. Its itinerary also included a cautious visit to the politically unstable areas of the Middle East before travelling via Nicosia to Ankara for the benefit of Turkish Airlines. On 26 July the Viscount arrived back at Wisley after another successful tour, which was undoubtedly responsible for a considerable number of new orders in the months ahead.

By this time an element of eager anticipation was growing within BEA, because the time was drawing close when the first production aircraft would be making its maiden flight. Prior to this important landmark the national carrier announced that it had

signed a contract for a further six Viscounts, thereby taking its future fleet total to 26. This latest order meant that Vickers now had firm commitments for 48 aircraft; a figure likely to change rapidly because the company had also received serious inquiries for 50 aircraft from various operators around the world.

On 20 August, BEA's first Viscount (G-ALWE) carried out its maiden sortie from Weybridge, the flight following the normal pattern by terminating at Wisley. A day earlier, its two-year old relative (G-AMAV) had been loaned to the Corporation by its owners, the Ministry of Supply, so that some preliminary route proving could be undertaken. No time was to be lost in starting the 200hr planned session, so the aircraft left London for Cyprus almost immediately, the first destination chosen for the series. Thereafter 'MAV was to be found on BEA's routes to Gibraltar, Madrid, Nice, Oslo, Stockholm and Vienna as well as a number of training visits to Shannon.

In the previous two years the prototype V700 had been shown at Farnborough, but in 1952 it was possible to delegate the newly-flown production machine for the week-long duties. Inspection in the static confirmed that it was externally identical to 'MAV, while the cabin interior layout had been finalised with 43 seats. Strangely enough, these were manufactured by Rumbold, whereas those installed in the Ambassador were produced by Vickers. Rumour had it that another 10 aircraft had been ordered, but this was neither confirmed nor denied by the sales team on site. During the course of its energetic flying demonstration, 'LWE whistled along the flight line happily relying upon the motive power derived from only one Dart. While not a practice to be recommended, the ability to remain aloft in such a situation must have brought comfort to some onlookers. Certainly it proved invaluable in January 1956 when a BEA specimen was forced to land at Cazaux, near Bordeaux, having lost the use of three engines. Subsequently it was found that salt water had contaminated the fuel taken on board during the aircraft's turn-round at Gibraltar.

After its lively performances at Farnborough, 'LWE returned to its test schedule, until in November 1952, the Air Registration Board (ARB) issued a certificate that allowed a maximum take-off weight of 56,000lb, 6,000lb more than called for in the original specification. Much of the flying was carried out by seconded BEA crews so that they could gain first-hand type experience, while other personnel from the Corporation were engaged in development and proving flights over the Mediterranean and Scandinavia with the V700. The latter was also used for a week-long tour of German cities from 23 September, carrying 750 passengers during the course of 18 demonstration sorties.

Above:
Iraqi Airways was suitably impressed by the visit of the prototype and duly placed an order, YI-ACK being the first to be delivered in 1955. After over 20 years' service, it was sold to Alidair as G-BFMW. *Via M. J. Hooks*

Below:
Not only did Trans-Canada become the first North American customer for the Viscount, but the airline also operated the later and larger Vanguard. *Via AJW*

It goes without saying that throughout this period the Vickers' sales team had not been idle in North America. Without a doubt, it was an uphill struggle because of the traditional support given to the home-based aviation industry, but in November, a significant breakthrough was finally achieved. Trans-Canada Airlines (TCA) ordered 15 Viscounts. The airline made its choice after many months of technical investigation and analysis, during which the economics and performance claims were compared with the US alternatives. The Convair 340 was the most favoured of the competitors, but the advances offered by the turboprop convinced the Canadian carrier that the British design would prove advantageous in the battle for passengers.

Once the contract had been signed, Vickers began work on the multitude of detailed design variations necessary to meet the severe TCA requirements. Obviously the aircraft would be operated in the extreme conditions of a Canadian winter, so the manufacturer had to provide additional heating in the passenger, crew and freight compartments. Some form of safeguard to protect the aircraft from the effects of frozen slush on runways had to be devised, while the electrical system needed more power if it was to cope with the additional demand.

Most of the remaining modifications were required on the flightdeck, where the customer not only wanted US instrumentation, but also a complete change of layout so that the aircraft could be flown at any time by a single crew member. All the equipment on the left and right consoles therefore had to be placed so that it could be reached by either pilot, the only suitable spot being on the roof panel. Other changes included the provision of a wiper on the central screen and enlarging the clearview panels. The latter was not done so that the hardy Canadian pilots could thrust a head out of the window while on final approach, but merely to allow them to do so when ground-starting rather than rely on an assortment of mysterious hand signals from engineers and others. Many of the alterations were steadily built into the V700 prototype, until in early 1953, G-AMAV finally shed the BEA livery it had always worn so that it could proudly display both the type and company's name in a prominent position on the fuselage. All was ready for a practical check of the redesigned features completed to date.

Accordingly, on Friday 13 February 1953, 'MAV set off from Wisley on the first leg of its journey to Montreal and its forthcoming chilly detachment. Perhaps not the best of days for the superstitious, especially when it was learned that bad weather made it impossible to land at Stornoway as intended. No doubt there was a certain relief when the wheels were firmly planted on Prestwick's runway instead. It was not until the early hours of Monday morning that conditions had sufficiently improved, to allow the Viscount to resume its journey over the next 856 miles (1,377km) stage to Keflavik, Iceland. With the programme now proceeding normally, 'MAV duly reached its Canadian destination on 17 February to complete the first Atlantic crossing by a turboprop aircraft.

Two days before the V700's departure from the UK, a ceremony involving the first production machine was held at Wisley. In those days it was the national carrier's practice to allocate class names to the various types in the fleet. The Viscount was no exception, so a competition was held amongst the staff to find a suitable identity for the latest addition. When the nose of 'LWE was anointed with the customary beverage by Lady Douglas, wife of BEA's Chairman, the inscription revealed that Discovery had been chosen as the theme for the type. It was thought appropriate because the Viscount would be breaking new ground in the advance of civil air transport. Each

Left:
BA aircraft entered service with BAF with little change in livery but with the new owner's logo substituted. *BAF*

subsequent specimen was therefore named after an explorer, but although the required number of suitable illustrious gentlemen were selected, the airline was unsuccessful in its attempt to market the aircraft by its class name. After a relatively short period, the Corporation sensibly decided to revert to 'Viscount', itself a name of some distinction.

At least the time was not wasted on 11 February, because in addition to the formal christening performance, the occasion was also used to announce the launch of a stretched version of the Viscount to be known as the V801. Since the Chairman of BEA was also present complete with pen and ink, the opportunity was taken to acquire his signature for 12 of this latest variant. On the whole, February 1953 was a very satisfactory month for Vickers.

Meanwhile, three more machines had left the Weybridge line and were actively engaged in route proving for their owner, BEA. However, production was not confined to building up the UK carrier's fleet, because the first of 12 for Air France was

about to appear from the assembly shed. Registered F-BGNK, the V708 took off from its birthplace on 11 March, just two years after the airline had placed its order. A swift count of the number of sales confirmed revealed that there was now a total of 66 on the books, but Vickers was confident that this figure would quickly grow once the Viscount proved itself in airline service.

There was not long to wait, because on 18 April the world's first regular scheduled service was flown by a turboprop airliner. This distinction was accorded G-AMNY, which left Heathrow bound for Cyprus with Capts A. S. Johnson and A. Wilson on the flightdeck. Staging through Rome and Athens, the final leg to Nicosia was actually flown on charter

Below:
BEA's first regular scheduled Viscount service was flown by G-AMNY on 18 April 1953. *AJW*

Above:
Hunting's third Viscount (G-AOGH) seen under construction, was the last of the 45 Type 700s to be built at Weybridge. Thereafter the aircraft were produced at Hurn. *Via D. M. Stroud*

Below:
The prototype V700 replaced G-AMNZ as the BEA entry for the New Zealand race in 1953. *AJW*

to Cyprus Airways, which normally operated this sector of BEA's twice-weekly service. Istanbul was added to the type's duties on the following day, with the result that the Corporation's two longest routes were now flown by the Viscount. Only a few weeks later there were sufficient aircraft available to introduce the Swiss destinations to the growing network, at the same time offering a reduction in fares. In fact, at the end of the first month of operation it was reported that the five machines on strength had completed 610hr of flying over 136,000 miles, carrying some 5,000 passengers in the process. When announcing these figures, the airline's chief executive also added that the Viscount would be introduced on the London-Glasgow and Belfast domestic routes from the start of the forthcoming winter season.

In May 1953, a new category of customer joined the list. Until this point national carriers had been in the forefront, but towards the end of the month independent Hunting Air Transport indicated that it was to order three V732s for use on its scheduled services. This lead was soon followed by Airwork, but in neither case were the companies able to employ their modern equipment in a profitable manner. There was a distinct impression given by the authority of the day that it considered that fast and comfortable aircraft were not appropriate to non-flag carriers' operations. Seemingly only slow, obsolescent types carrying a maximum number of hard seats were suitable. Inevitably it was not long before the Viscounts were either leased or sold to eager foreign carriers.

Some five years earlier the idea of an air race between London and New Zealand had been mooted. At the outset the prospect aroused considerable interest and a healthy provisional list of would-be participants, but as the years passed, so the numbers dwindled. Amongst those remaining in the handicap section was a Viscount 701 belonging to BEA, the entrant being the appropriately registered and named G-AMNZ *James Cook*. Unfortunately, it was found impossible to release the aircraft from its normal duties, so reluctantly the Corporation was forced to consider withdrawing from the race. With such a small field, this was certainly thought undesirable by the organisers, so a request was made to the Ministry of Supply to loan the V700 prototype to the airline. Therefore, after a fairly brief spell in Vickers' colours, the aircraft found itself back in BEA's livery with the addition of the name *Endeavour* and racing number 23. Surprisingly, time was still found for 'MAV to join Air France's F-BGNN at Farnborough during the then annual SBAC show.

When the day dawned for the start of the race on 8 October 1953, the total number of aircraft at the line-up had dropped to eight; five of them Canberras in the speed division. Of the three transports,

the Viscount's progress was likely to be watched with greatest interest in view of it being the only turboprop entered. Intended as a medium-range aircraft, it was not ideally suited to racing half-way round the world against the larger, long-range DC-6A representing KLM. With this in mind, the BEA team planned to take the least possible time to complete the course, aided by a number of useful modifications to 'MAV. Four Marston Excelsior bag fuel tanks were installed in the cabin to take the machine's total capacity to 2,850gal. This reduced the number of transit stops to four (Bahrain, Negombo, Cocos and Melbourne) with the latter sector being the longest leg of 3,499 miles. Some remarkable refuelling times were achieved by all concerned; those for the Viscount varying between 14min at Bahrain and 22min at Cocos.

Despite covering the course to Christchurch in an elapsed time of 40hr 41min, as expected, the Vickers turboprop was soundly beaten on handicap by the DC-6A. Nevertheless, its performance was excellent with some impressive speeds recorded throughout the journey. Of course, for the purposes of the exercise the all-up weight was increased to 64,800lb, compared with the 56,000lb for the standard aircraft of the type and the original design figure of 45,000lb. Nonetheless, the demonstration of reliability was worth far more to the manufacturer than the prize money.

Unlike the famous 1934 MacRobertson to Australia, the 1953 London-Christchurch race generated little public interest. It lacked the pioneering characters and the variety of types involved 20 years earlier, not to mention the disappointing number of entrants. In this respect it was unsuccessful, yet it did at least provide an excellent platform for the aviation industry to display its wares.

Prior to the race Vickers continued to receive a steady flow of orders, albeit in small batches. As more Viscounts entered airline service, so the operating economics and the enormous passenger appeal convinced those hesitating that it was essential to join the queue. Anticipating an increased demand, Vickers decided to set up another production line at Bournemouth (Hurn), a facility already leased from the Government. Work started in December 1953, with the Viscount replacing the Varsity in the extensive accommodation which was sufficiently large to contain two assembly lines. In due course the Hurn factory was developed so that it also possessed its own design and test facilities, eventually being responsible for the construction of 279 of the 445 Viscounts produced. At one stage six aircraft per month were being completed at the plant, which when added to the Weybridge figures, took the overall total to 10, an unprecedented rate for a British civil transport.

At the end of the year BEA released some statistics for the type's first six months of operation

Delivered in 1956, the V745D N7441 served with Capital for five years before the United take-over.
G. W. Pennick

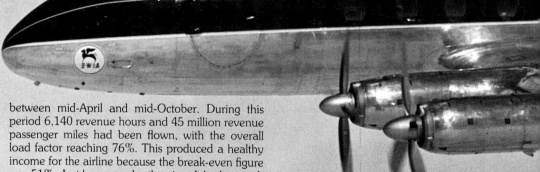

Below:

In later years G-AMAV was repainted into various customers' colours, in this case British West Indian Airways.
Via M. J. Hooks

between mid-April and mid-October. During this period 6,140 revenue hours and 45 million revenue passenger miles had been flown, with the overall load factor reaching 76%. This produced a healthy income for the airline because the break-even figure was 51%. Just how popular the aircraft had proved, was illustrated by the dramatic rise in passenger numbers on the highly-competitive routes flown by the Viscount. For instance, on the London-Istanbul and Zurich services BEA's share of the traffic rose from 34% to 54%, while on the Geneva run the gain averaged 23%. An encouraging set of results indeed, but the chairman emphasised that they were achieved during the peak summer months and could be adversely affected during the coming winter.

When TCA had opted for the turboprop airliner in late 1952, it was hoped that its entry into North America would stimulate the attention of US carriers. In the spring of 1954 this reaction was still awaited, but at least some preparatory work was in hand. At the request of the ARB, the US Civil Aero-nautics Administration (CAA, later FAA, Federal Aviation Agency) dispatched four of its officials to Britain to commence the certification procedures. A Viscount was placed at the team's disposal, with some of the visitors' programme arranged so that some experience was gained of the type in actual airline service. Although no definite orders had been received, Vickers believed that there were now several US operators interested, making CAA approval an important first step. It was a wise move because in early June the long-awaited breakthrough was made. Capital Airlines had placed an order.

True, it involved a contract for only three aircraft, but the airline also took an option on a further 37 machines, increasing the value of the order to some 45 million (about £16 million). Capital's network was entirely domestic and was maintained by some 0 DC-3s, DC-4s and Constellations. The choice of the Viscount therefore meant that a major re-equipment exercise was contemplated, which, when completed, would provide the airline with a much-expanded capacity. Initially it was thought that the US carrier wished to carry out some cautious operational evaluation with the token trio before fully committing itself, but this was not the case. Principally the hesitation was used to test the general public's reaction to the decision, which was actually received with far greater enthusiasm than had been expected. Helpfully, BEA agreed to postpone its last three deliveries, so these were the first to cross the Atlantic rather than the developed version specified by Capital.

Encouraged by the favourable market research results, the company decided to take up the 37 options in August 1954 without waiting for the trial aircraft to arrive. There was

allocated to the task of bringing the type to US standards. Fortunately, many of the changes were amongst the 250 demanded at the time of the TCA order, but those outstanding involved a fuel-jettisoning facility, integral airstairs, strengthened wing spars, a redesigned nose for weather radar and an efficient air-conditioning system. The latter was particularly vital in view of the extremely hot climate on some of the US routes, because it had already been proved that the Viscount's large windows tended to produce a green-house effect. A formidable list, but one which Vickers completed to the satisfaction of all concerned, culminating in the hand over of the CAA Type Certificate by the US officials at a short

ceremony in London on 13 June 1955. Thereafter all V700s ordered with the same features as the much-modified, Dart RDa 6 Mk 510-powered TCA and Capital machines, automatically acquired a 'D' suffix to their Type number.

The news of the order had shocked the US aircraft industry, but none more so than Consolidated-Vultee, the manufacturers of the rival Cv340. A series of misleading statements were promptly issued, each comparing the Viscount's performance unfavourably with that of its own product. Without doubt the company was alarmed by the prospect of other major carriers choosing to support the foreign product, a situation which was almost unknown. Although the 340 was a fine aircraft, the fact remained that it was piston-engined; a powerplant which had become obsolescent with the introduction of the turboprop.

This was of little consolation to Convair, but at least Capital would not be introducing the upstart for another year. Meanwhile, across the border in Canada, TCA was nearing the point when its first machines would be delivered. With crew training completed in the early New Year, there were sufficient aircraft on strength to allow a pre-inaugural service on 23 February 1955. Flying from Toronto to New York, the V724 CF-TGI carried members of the press on the trip which lasted 1hr 39min, compared with the two hours taken by the

also a pleasant surprise in store because the airline also took options on another 20 Viscounts, which, if confirmed, would begin to appear in 1957. Until this point Capital had never ordered new short/medium-range aircraft despite flying sectors averaging only 297 miles. Instead, it had found it economically preferable to employ long-haul equipment on short stages.

It always seems a little strange that opinions differ from country to country when certifying aircraft. After all, the common objective is for the utmost safety, yet some authorities insist on modifications thought non-essential by their counterparts elsewhere. In the case of the Viscount, Vickers had to incorporate 26 additional features into the design before it met the CAA's requirements. This did not include some extra items specified by the customer, so altogether a vast number of man-hours were

DC-4Ms normally employed on the route. American Airlines had already anticipated the faster flights by substituting DC-6s on to its competing schedules, which then matched the times offered by the turboprop. TCA was therefore hopeful that the novelty value alone would help to regain the customers lost to the US carrier. When commercial services began on 1 April, the first to benefit was the Montreal-Toronto-Lakehead-Winnipeg route; quickly followed by the Montreal-New York sector on the 4 April. The Viscount was an overnight success wherever it flew, but particularly so on the routes across the border.

When Capital started its operations between Washington and Chicago on 26 July 1955, the airline could therefore hardly fail. At first three daily flights were provided, two of which made the trip non-stop, but as deliveries gathered momentum, so the coverage increased throughout the densely populated New York-Chicago-Pittsburgh triangle and south to New Orleans. During the first 90 days of service, load factors averaged over 90% with some 10,000hr flown by the Darts without one malfunction. Capital was soon back as top carrier in the region, a position it had not held since 1947/48. Sadly it was not enough. Its ambitious expansion plans had caused the company to over-reach itself and in 1960 United took over the ailing operator. Capital placed the blame for its downfall on the Vis-

count, but in reality it was the airliner which was largely responsible for assisting the carrier through a difficult period. This was certainly confirmed by the new owner because it continued to operate the type with great success for a further 10 years.

Naturally, Northeast Airlines had observed the surge in traffic on routes served by the Viscount, so in an effort to enjoy similar benefits, the carrier placed an order with Vickers for 10 V798s. Eight of these were readily available, having been built as V745Ds for Capital but subsequently cancelled before delivery. After conversion at Hurn, deliveries began in the summer of 1958 to enable services to begin on the Washington-New York-Boston sectors. Almost immediately Northeast's market share rose from 8% to 15%, with load factors maintaining an average of 60% into the 1960s.

Despite the availability of the larger Models, Vickers continued to receive orders for the Type 700, although the later machines were all fitted with Dart 510s. Similarly most of the earlier aircraft were re-engined with Mk 506s to bring them up to the more advanced standard. It was with considerable reluctance that the airlines were eventually obliged to retire the type from first line services as the presence of the modern jets began to take effect. Many of the aircraft were rejuvenated for a new career as executive transports, while others continued in commercial service in other parts of the world.

Right:
Although originally intended for Capital as N7470, when the order was cancelled the aircraft was converted for Northeast and re-registered N6590C.
R. S. Armstrong via G. W. Pennick

Below:
United Steel bought the Viscount 764D new in December 1956 as N907.
L. Smalley via G. W. Pennick

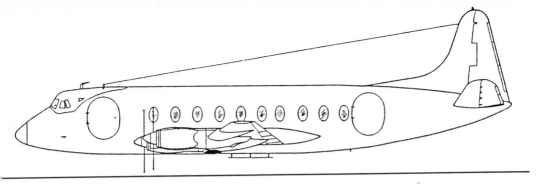

The Type 800

Even before the V700 series had entered service, the Vickers design team had already turned its attention towards further development of the Viscount. One of the aims was to increase the size of the passenger accommodation, but at the same time improve the operating economics. Traditionally this was usually achieved by lengthening the fuselage; a satisfactory solution in most cases. Vickers offered this proposal to BEA in 1952 since the Corporation was keen to acquire a larger version of the newcomer. After checking the numerous facts and figures against its own sums, BEA decided to order 12 of the variant now known as the Type 800. Following the familiar Vickers' system for identifying its customers, the airline's batch was allocated V801 and the contract was prepared to receive the signature of Lord Douglas of Kirtleside. This event was organised to take place on the occasion of the naming of BEA's first V701 at Weybridge on 11 February 1953.

In order to meet the requirement for more capacity, the newcomer's fuselage was lengthened by 13ft 3in (4.04m), giving the expanded cabin the capability of carrying 86 tourist class seats. Development of the Dart was progressing in parallel at Rolls-Royce, so the more powerful RDa 5 giving 1,690ehp for take-off was chosen to drive the V801. It was intended to complement the V701 in BEA's service by taking over the short/medium range sectors on the busier routes. These included the Belfast, Edinburgh and Glasgow domestic flights plus international sorties to Amsterdam, Brussels, Dusseldorf, Geneva, Nice and Zurich. However, as time passed, it became apparent that the engine was not really suitable for the much-enlarged aircraft which had a gross weight of 65,000lb (29,484kg). Estimated performance figures indicated that the cruising speed would be less than that of the V701; hardly an encouraging prospect.

It was a view shared by both Vickers and the Corporation which led to the cancellation of the latter's order for the V801. This was virtually a formality because in the meantime the manufacturer had been working on a modified version tailored to meet the needs of BEA. With the more suitable alternative design mutually agreed, the airline placed an order for 12 Viscount Majors (the name it used to refer to the aircraft) in April 1954. Although larger than the V701, the fuselage had been given a more modest stretch of only 3ft 10in (1.17m), but at the same time the rear pressure bulkhead was moved aft by 5ft 5in (1.66m). By so doing, the cabin length was extended by 9ft 3in (2.81m) thereby providing space for additional rows of seats, the precise number depending upon the layout required.

The revised fuselage contained several new features, all aimed to give maximum freight and passenger flexibility plus easier loading of bulky items of cargo. For the latter purpose the forward entrance door was enlarged to 5ft x 4ft (1.52m x 1.22m) and changed to a rectangular shape instead of the familiar oval pattern chosen for the 700 series. From experience it had been found that the latter could be difficult to operate in windy conditions, so the opportunity was taken to revert to a more orthodox door design which would lay flat against the fuselage when open. The rear entrance was also given a similarly shaped, but smaller, replacement door. Both the galley and forward bulkhead were mounted on rails so that the size of the freight area could be readily adjusted. When 70 passengers were to be carried, 12 rows of seats were arranged in a five-abreast formation, two rows containing two either side of the aisle, while at the extreme rear one pair made up the total. In a 58-seat mode there were 14 rows arranged four abreast plus the one extra pair, while for extreme comfort only 11 rows of four seats were installed

Right:
**A typical interior of a BEA
Viscount 802.** *AJW*

Below right:
**The more austere cabin of a
Viking used for charter work
in the 1960s.** *AJW*

Below:
**A party spirit can prevail in
the starboard front seats of a
Viscount.** *BAF*

when the aircraft was employed on first class services.

This time the Dart RDa 6 Mk 510 was available, the developed engine being rated at 1,740ehp for take-off at a maximum weight of 64,500lb (29,257kg). It was able to propel the Viscount at 325mph in the cruise, a more acceptable figure than that quoted for the V801. There was little doubt that the variant was a far more attractive proposition than the discarded project, its specification making it more valuable to the manufacturer for export and other sales. This was soon confirmed by KLM when it broke a long association with the US industry by placing an order for nine V803s, a notable success indeed for Vickers. It was planned that 53 passengers would be carried: 16 in the forward, first class section, plus a tourist cabin containing 37 seats.

Although the 802 had still to appear, in mid-May 1955 BEA reconfirmed its confidence in the type by placing an order for another 10 examples plus one V701. The latter was required to replace Ambassador G-AMAB which had been written off in a forced landing near Dusseldorf on 8 April. At this time the airline was suffering from a shortage of aircraft due to the need to take the V701s out of service progressively for modifications to be completed. Four members of the fleet were also grounded because they had suffered damage of varying seriousness.

At the beginning of 1956, yet another order was placed by the Corporation. During the past year a new three turbine-stage Dart was introduced as the RDa 7 Mk 520, so it was selected to power the V806. BEA specified a 58-seat interior for the 19

aircraft, which otherwise were identical to the V802. Aer Lingus followed suit in May by ordering six V808s, a total destined to be greatly increased in the 1960s by the purchase of both Eagle's and KLM's retired fleets.

By April 1956, the fuselage of the first V802 was installed in the new assembly sheds at Weybridge after its construction at Hurn. With the latter plant now fully operational, it had become responsible for all main series 700 assembly work and the production of both 700 and 800 series fuselages. All 800 and the future 810 assembly was earmarked for Weybridge, with construction of the component parts shared with Hurn. An important milestone had also been passed because altogether, orders for the various models now exceeded 300.

On 27 July the first of the larger Viscounts made its maiden flight; the V802 G-AOJA staying aloft for 55min before landing at Wisley. Although technically considered a prototype, the aircraft was destined to be the flagship of the eventual BEA fleet. For the next month or so Juliet Alpha was flown with test equipment occupying most of the cabin, but this was removed for the duration of its presence at Farnborough in September. Here it was possible to note the new arrangement of the instrument panel and the permanent position of the Decca Flight Log on the flightdeck. There were also some alterations to the main cabin's appearance,

Below:
Deliveries of KLM's V803s began in 1957 with PH-VIG arriving in November. Nine years later it became EI-AOM with Aer Lingus, but crashed into the Irish Sea in March 1968. *G. W. Pennick*

but generally the only obvious differences from the V701 rested with the additional windows and rectangular doors.

With only the final phase of the flight trials outstanding, the first V802 was formally accepted by BEA on 27 November. It had been decided to continue the Discovery class established by the earlier V701s, once again using names that presumably took considerable research to discover. For instance, the nose of G-AOJA revealed that Sir Samuel White Baker had been chosen in this case, duly confirmed by Lady Douglas of Kirtleside as she carried out the ceremonial duties. No doubt she was aware of the gentleman's achievements, but it seems unlikely that many of the aircraft's future passengers would recall that he discovered Albert Nyanza in the Nile basin in 1864 and later commanded an expedition to the Sudan under the Khedive. Sadly Sir Samuel's mount crashed at Belfast

on 23 October 1957 after a total flying time of only 1,472hr.

During the course of the event it was recalled that when the V701 flagship was named in February 1953, 42 orders for the Viscount had been received but none delivered. This total had risen to 200 at the time of the hand-over of the first Capital machine in mid-1955 with 55 aircraft in the customers' possession. Some 18 months later 357 had been ordered of which 156 had been delivered. Of these, 152 were in regular operation and the type was still the only turbine-powered aircraft in passenger service outside the USSR.

In January 1957 the V802 was awarded its certificate, so within a matter of days BEA received the first member of the new fleet. This was soon joined by another five of its brethren, allowing the airline to inaugurate services on 18 February. Four return passenger trips and one freight run were flown between London and Paris that day, to form a modest introduction for the V802 on selected European and domestic routes. A time of 1hr 10min was allowed for the journey between the two capitals, 15min less than that taken by the Ambassadors previously employed. For some time, the latter had been in competition with the Viscounts of Air France, which had tended to favour the foreign carrier in terms of load factors. BEA now hoped to reverse the trend.

Right:
V806 cabin interior looking forward. The seat covers are blue as installed by British Airways. *BAF*

Below:
The prototype Viscount 802 G-AOJA was useful for sheltering from the rain at the 1956 SBAC show. *AJW*

As more V802s came on strength, the French sector was steadily built up until 11 services per day were flown in April, the month that Dublin, Belfast and Frankfurt were also added to the coverage. By the end of July, the variant was also to be found on other schedules to Amsterdam, Brussels, Copenhagen, Dusseldorf, Geneva, Nice and Zurich, not to mention the Glasgow and Edinburgh trunk routes. Even the regular sorties to Milan with freight were entrusted to the newcomers, thereby taking full advantage of the design's flexibility. Obviously by taking over these duties other aircraft had been released. In some cases it enabled the V701s and Ambassadors to be redeployed and for a start to be made upon the gradual disposal of the latter type.

Meanwhile, construction of the first V806 was well advanced at Weybridge, with the first flight scheduled for the summer. Due to its close relationship to the V802, the necessary test work was not expected to be too protracted so BEA was confidently anticipating service entry well before the end of the year. Although registered to the airline, when G-AOYF flew on 9 August in Vickers' livery it carried the information on the fuselage that it was a Viscount 806-810. The manufacturer had retained the aircraft for the C of A programme of the V810 as a temporary expedient until a replacement was available. At this point Yankee Fox was due to revert to V806 standard before joining the Corporation. As a result of this rearrangement, the second machine off the line (G-AOYG) became BEA's first V806 soon after its first flight on 4 October.

Although the V802/806 variants were excellent aircraft, total sales of the series only reached 67, all going to customers in Europe apart from those acquired by New Zealand National Airways.

Right:
Later the cabin interiors were modernised to give a wide body impression. *BAF*

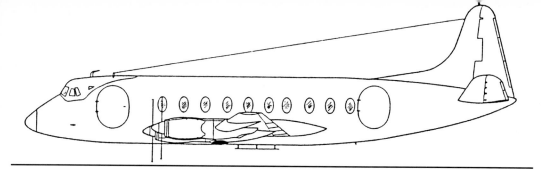

The Type 810

At an early stage in the development of the essentially short-haul V800 series, Vickers was aware that there was a need for a machine with the same capacity but able to fly faster over longer distances; a capability which would doubtless appeal to many airlines. Already Continental Airlines in the US had expressed an interest, especially after monitoring the traffic figures enjoyed by Capital following the introduction of the Viscount in 1955.

Before such a machine could be contemplated, a suitable powerplant had to be found. This created few problems because, as on earlier occasions, Rolls-Royce already had the solution. The engine manufacturer had further developed the three-stage RDa 7 fitted to the V806 so that yet more power was available from the new RDa 7/1 Mk 525. This latest offering could produce 2,100ehp for take-off, but it was derated for Viscount purposes to 1,990ehp otherwise the Darts might have taken off without the aircraft. The spare power source therefore made an ideal reserve for operations from hot

and high airfields. Although it was basically similar to the Mk 520 engine, the more advanced version contained several new features including higher flame temperatures, recalibrated fuel controls and an additional pitch stop for the propeller.

Having agreed on the powerplant, the next step was to design an airframe to match the performance. There was no need to look beyond the basic 800 series, which, together with its smaller Type 700 relative, had successfully completed over one million operating hours. Naturally a certain amount of strengthening was necessary for the higher weights and speeds envisaged for the aircraft, by this time designated the Type 810, but the

Below:
Continental Airlines was the first customer for the V810 when ordering 15 of the variant. Delivered in March 1959, N252V later became G-APPU with Channel Airways until it ran out of runway at Southend. *L. Smalley via G. W. Pennick*

dimensions remained the same. While numerous minor structural improvements had been progressively incorporated during the service life of early Viscounts, the changes introduced into the V810 were the first of a major nature. As a result the fatigue properties of the airframe were considerably improved during the work on load-bearing components such as the wing spar and rib. Another area to receive attention was around the rear fuselage and fin, so that the increased loads imposed by an asymmetric take-off could be safely handled.

In order to cope with the increased weight, it was necessary to provide a strengthened undercarriage complete with an enhanced braking system, particularly since the aircraft would be expected to have a good short-field performance. Rudder power was increased by using larger deflections, while better elevator control was achieved with a redesigned spring tab assembly. This allowed the existing centre of gravity range to be retained with the more powerful engines. Past experience had shown that the gaps between the control surfaces and the vertical and horizontal tail structure were too large, often resulting in an accumulation of snow. A closer fit considerably reduced the effect of this unwelcome feature. All of the improvements were gradually added to the prototype V700, G-AMAV, to enable the general handling qualities to be examined. While operating at low weights and with uprated Dart RDa 7s, the machine was regularly flown at 400mph without a hint of protest.

Continental was sufficiently impressed by the promise of the V810 to place an order for 15 in December 1955, the first to be received by Vickers. Although much of the early test flying had been carried out by 'MAV, it was essential to have a more representative airframe available at an early date. With the full agreement of BEA, the latter's initial

V806 was completed to V810 standard with the more powerful engines and first flown on 9 August 1957. Trials immediately began, with the aim of gaining the type certificate as soon as possible. To comply with the requirements, the evaluation of the aircraft's performance in tropical conditions necessitated a trip to Africa in September with special clearance for operation at a weight of 69,000lb.

The progress of the V810 then suffered a temporary set-back, because on 20 October, 'OYF was badly damaged at Johannesburg while in the process of making a simulated emergency landing. A heavier-than-intended impact with the runway caused the collapse of the starboard undercarriage, which in turn affected the wing and engines. A fire in one of the latter was quickly extinguished, but the cumulative effect meant that it was not worth considering repairs. Sadly the demonstration had proved too realistic but fortunately there were no casualties. In due course the mortal remains were leisurely returned to Weybridge by sea, to be eventually rebuilt as a standard V806 for BEA. When delivered as G-APOX, it had the distinction of becoming the last Viscount to join the airline.

While the V700 prototype was suitable for some of the trials, Vickers had to wait another two months for the first purpose-built V810 to fly from Weybridge as G-AOYV on 23 December. This time the trials proceeded without a further hitch, to conclude with the award of the FAA Type Certificate on 22 April 1958. Deliveries to Continental began during the following month, so that on 28 May the airline became the second major American domestic carrier to operate the Viscount. Much of the airline's route network was spread over the central and southern area of the US, but the first sector to be flown by the newcomers was the link between Chicago and Los Angeles. The turboprop airliner aroused considerable interest at the Californian airport because the type was still virtually unknown on the west coast.

Continental's V812s were configured with 52 seats to enable a very comfortable two-abreast arrangement to be offered. An eight-seat cabin was located between the two-crew flightdeck and the forward toilets, while at the extreme rear of the aircraft, a four-seat lounge was provided aft of the galley. Such a facility was previously the exclusive preserve of long-haul types, so the provision in a short/medium range airliner caused something of a sensation at the time. The feature was also specified by some other customers of the V810 in due course, but alternatively the space could be employed for freight. Retractable airstairs were fitted at the forward passenger entrance, these being a similar type to those successfully installed in the Capital machines. By redesigning the interior trim of the V812, the cabin was in effect made 4in wider, which was certainly useful when considering a five-abreast layout.

One of the criterion for Continental when selecting the V812 in the first instance was its ability to operate out of Denver, the 5,000ft-above sea level location of the company's headquarters. Elsewhere the Viscounts had to contend with high temperatures, so a wide range of operating conditions were imposed upon the aircraft. Take-off weight was 67,500lb (30,6198kg) with a payload of 15,000lb (6,804kg), which it could carry on stages up to 1,100 miles (1,770km) in length, at a cruising speed of 365mph. It was not long before the US carrier recognised that the V812 was proving to be the most economic type in its fleet, despite being operated in a first class mode. The break-even figure was found to be an easily attainable 38%, but in the face of growing competition from the jets, the

Viscounts were relegated to the airline's secondary routes by the end of the decade. In 1966 Continental decided it was time to dispose of the remaining fleet members, which had already been reduced to 11 specimens after sales and crashes. The entire collection was acquired by the Southend-based Channel Airways, whereupon the aircraft were ferried across the Atlantic during the early months of 1967. Needless to say, the first class interiors were soon removed to be replaced by the high-density seating for which the UK airline was renowned.

For much of its early career with the manufacturer, the prototype ('OYV) was painted in Continental's livery while employed on its demonstration and test duties. One of its tasks in 1959 resulted in it flying with a Vanguard shaped vertical tail complete with the Napier Spraymat de-icing system intended for the new type. Later, as Viscount development began to decline, the V810 was found to be surplus to requirements, so Vickers sold the machine to the Brasilian carrier VASP in 1960.

Undoubtedly the V810 was an advanced design for its time and attracted a number of orders from carriers around the world, often from operators of V700s keen to update their fleets. It proved to be more popular than the earlier 800 series, with 84 examples being sold before the final Viscount to be delivered joined the Chinese carrier, CAAC, on 16 April 1964. Although no new aircraft were to appear, the type continued to be a popular choice of many companies in the second-hand market.

Below:
The prototype V810 (G-AOYV) carried Continental livery for much of its test career, even when used by Vickers for Vanguard development work.
Via M. J. Hooks

47

The Dart

In the immediate postwar period, the speed with which the pure-jet engines had been designed and tested encouraged a general wave of optimism. Progress was not quite so smooth for the turboprop because there was the added complication of the airscrew reduction gear and control, while in some cases the centrifugal compressor was replaced by the more complex and delicate axial-flow unit. In fact, elation was quickly replaced by gloom when the turbojet's successes were not shared by the propeller variant. As development work continued, there were few signs of any marked changes in the situation. A succession of problems were experienced with the engines including reduction gear failures, combustion chamber disintegration and impeller cracks. Weights were far too high, as indeed was the fuel consumption. To complete the picture of depression the power output was unacceptably low.

The Dart was going through all these phases as Vickers was preparing its Viscount design. Work on the turboprop had begun in 1945 and the first engine ran in the summer of the following year with disappointing results. Even in 1947 there were doubts about the engine's future and alternatives were seriously being considered by the Ministry. This meant that although Vickers firmly supported the Rolls-Royce powerplant, it was obliged to prepare a brochure in 1947 outlining the V640 Viscount project complete with its four Napier Naiads. The criticism of the Dart continued throughout the year, many inferring that the airliner would merely become a testbed and never enter service.

In August, the Ministry appeared to be convinced that there was a distinct improvement in the Dart's performance, so it notified Vickers that it should be installed in the prototype, despite BEA's misgivings and preferences for piston engines or other types of

turboprops. By this time the much-maligned engine had been mounted in the nose of Lancaster NG465 for its airborne trials, which began on 10 October 1947. The initial results were most encouraging and confirmed that the worst of the problems had been overcome. This early version was known as the RDa 1 Mk 1 and had a rating of 1,125ehp at a maximum speed of 14,500rpm. In its civil guise it became the Mk 501, but it was soon superseded by the Mk 502 which had an improved performance yet ran 500rpm slower after shrouding the blade-tips of the two-stage turbine. Four of this version were installed in the prototype Viscount when it made its first flight in July 1948. By the time that the engine passed its second Air Registration Board type-test in September, the new Mk 503 was back at 14,500rpm. It was about this point in the Dart's development that the input side of the reduction assembly was changed to single-helical type gears

to eliminate a troublesome, high-frequency vibration.

Now that progress was gaining momentum, Rolls-Royce was able to offer the RDa 3 Mk 504 which had a much higher power output compared with its predecessor. Vickers designed the larger V700 around this engine and in August 1950 four of the series were installed in the prototype when it made its first flight. The turbine had been modified to improve its performance by increasing the capacity of the two-stage centrifugal compressor. This culminated in the Mk 505 production version for use in the V700s then coming off the line for BEA. With all the experience of the Mk 504 incorporated, it was introduced with an overhaul life of 400hr. Even this latest variant was soon replaced by the superior Mk 506, which produced even higher power when cruising with the assistance of polished, thinner-section rotating guide-vanes in the compressor. This

All Viscounts had their Darts enclosed in slimline nacelles.
L. Smalley via G. W. Pennick

engine then became the standard powerplant for the V700, until the advent of the RDa 6 Mk 510 needed to meet the increased performance demanded in the US and elsewhere.

This constituted a major step in development for the Dart because the unit possessed a bigger reduction-gear load capacity, a different gear ratio plus turbine-blade tip seals. These changes were naturally retained in the RDa 7 Mk 520 series which was the next to appear for use in the proposed V806. Since the RDa 6 was at its maximum loading consistent with high efficiency, it was necessary to add a third turbine-stage to absorb any extra power. Otherwise the engine retained the characteristic combustion chamber layout in which the seven individual cans were set at an angle to the axis in order to reduce the overall length.

After its rather uncertain start, the Dart became one of the most reliable powerplants of all time. At the end of the first five years in service statistics revealed that the failure rate was one in 80,000hr, whereas the comparable figure for piston-engines was about 10 times as great. Overhaul periods tended to vary, but some units had reached 2,000hr before they were removed from the aircraft for examination.

Throughout the Dart's test phases, the early in-flight work carried out by the Lancaster and Wellington LN715 was invaluable. The latter type was no stranger to such an occupation, because from 1942 several of the breed had uncomplainingly carried early turbojets aloft. Of course, in these cases the aircraft at least retained the normal mode of propulsion, whereas the Darts replaced both Hercules during the trials of the turboprop.

These early results had little bearing on actual airline operations. While estimates and theories flowed forth, they were no substitute for practical experience. This fact had not escaped BEA which was busily preparing for the introduction of its new V701s in 1953. The Corporation therefore decided to fit two DC-3s with Dart 505s to gain some knowledge of the operation and maintenance of the powerplant in everyday conditions. By using the aircraft on cargo flights, the carrier hoped to defray some of the cost of the research and development by the revenue earned.

Scottish Aviation converted G-ALXN and G-AMDB into freighters before they flew to Hucknall for the installation of the engines. These were the subject of a Ministry of Supply contract to Rolls-Royce as part of the RDa 3 development programme, which also covered overhauls and the supply of spares. Delivery of the first aircraft to be completed took place on 9 June 1951, when 'LXN was handed over to BEA together with a new C of A approving freight activities. Initially the aircraft was employed for training the crews allocated to the venture, but this became rather protracted due to maintenance delays. Staff shortages in the peak season meant that this additional workload was given a fairly low priority. Eventually it was possible to operate a proving flight between Northolt and Renfrew on 10/11 August which confirmed the feasibility of the plans already prepared for the future operation. The sortie was followed by the inaugural scheduled freight run to Bückeberg (Hanover) on 15 August, the world's first such service by a turboprop.

In September Rolls-Royce delivered the second machine; thereafter both aircraft continued flying until the onset of winter. During the next few months full air-intake and airscrew de-icing was fitted, since these items had been omitted from the original conversion due to a shortage of components. The few that were available were urgently needed for the Viscount prototypes. In the spring of 1952 other routes were added to the network flown by the Dart-Dakotas, including Copenhagen, Milan and Stockholm, all destinations intended to be a part of the Viscounts' itinerary in the future. These sectors gave a wide variety of operating conditions and produced valuable information about the engine's behaviour in both cold and hot environments.

The modified DC-3s carried the standard BEA fuel tankage of 680gal, which allowed a maximum range of 750 miles (1,206km) with a 4,350lb (1,973kg) payload.

Airframe limitations restricted the speed range, but 191mph was permissible at 5,000ft, increasing to 218mph at 20,000ft. Needless to say, the presence of a DC-3 at such altitudes was something of a shock to the nervous systems of military controllers. On more than one occasion fighters were scrambled to investigate the unidentified object ambling along over Europe. Conditions for flying the machine were also less than ideal, because the normally cramped flightdeck frequently had an extra member squeezed into the limited space as an observer. Never a quiet haven at the best of times, with the extended nacelles of the Darts placing the propellers in direct line with the windscreen, the level of noise was considerably higher than even that produced by a pair of Pratt & Whitneys rumbling away nearby.

Although the two DC-3s carried out their unusual duties very effectively, it was never intended that they would be retained on the freight services at the conclusion of the engine trials. To be economic it was necessary to operate at high altitudes, which severely limited the range of goods that could be carried in an unheated and unpressurised hold. Generally the Darts performed very well during this preparatory period of commercial service, with any

snags being relatively minor. Operations were due to end in October 1952, but in the event 'MDB was retained for a further 350hr flying into 1953. Both aircraft had been restored to their more usual powerplant and back in routine airline service by the end of the year, having played a valuable part in the future success of the Viscount.

Just as the Wellington, Lancaster and DC-3s helped with the Dart, so the Viscount itself played a similar role in the development of turboprop engines. Pratt & Whitney of Canada bought the retired V757 C-FTID from Air Canada in 1972 for conversion into a flying testbed for its products, the first to be installed being the PT6A-50. The work was carried out by by the manufacturer's Helicopter and Systems Division based at Quebec and involved the grafting of the new nacelle into the nose of the Viscount. A considerable amount of strengthening was required to carry the unit, which was a faithful replica of that intended for the Dash Seven then under development. Test flying did not start until 1974, but from this point regular sorties were made by the five-engined machine. Once the PT6A-50 had completed its trials, the testbed was prepared to accept other engines destined for such as the SD3-30 and similar aircraft.

Below:
Jersey has always proved a busy seasonal destination for the airlines. As the Rapides of the 1940s gave way to DC-3s in the 1950s, so the Viscount became a familiar sight for the next three decades. *AJW*

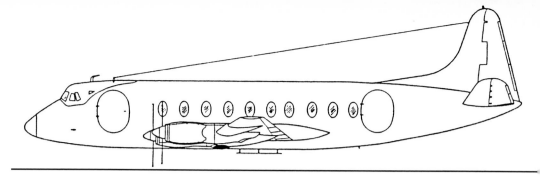

Variants

The following are series numbers within the basic 700/800/810 model ranges that were issued to Viscount customers by Vickers. Other than the few in the 600 block, only those aircraft actually completed are included in the list. There were others allocated that for one reason or another were not taken up. A 'D' suffix was given to the Type 700 machines fitted with Dart RDa 6 engines and the features incorporated at the time of the US certification.

Type number	Engines	Remarks
V609	Armstrong Siddeley Mamba	Brabazon Type IIB proposal
V630	Dart RDa 1 Mk 502	Prototype Viceroy/Viscount
V640	Napier Naiad	Not completed
V655	Dart RDa 3 Mk 505	Developed as V700
V663	Tay RTa 1 turbojets	Converted second prototype V630
V700	Dart RDa 3 Mk 504/505	Prototype
V701	Dart RDa 3 Mk 505/506	Production version for BEA
V702	Dart RDa 3 Mk 506	British West Indian Airways
V707	Dart RDa 3 Mk 506	Aer Lingus
V708	Dart RDa 3 Mk 505	Air France
V720	Dart RDa 3 Mk 506	Trans-Australia Airlines
V723	Dart RDa 3 Mk 506	VIP layout for Indian Air Force
V724	Dart RDa 3 Mk 506	Trans-Canada Airlines
V730	Dart RDa 3 Mk 506	VIP layout for Indian Air Force
V732	Dart RDa 3 Mk 506	Hunting-Clan
V734	Dart RDa 3 Mk 506	VIP layout for Pakistan Air Force
V735	Dart RDa 3 Mk 506	Iraqi Airways
V736	Dart RDa 3 Mk 506	Fred Olsen
V737	Dart RDa 3 Mk 506	VIP layout for Canadian Government
V739	Dart RDa 3 Mk 506	Misrair
V742D	Dart RDa 6 Mk 510	VIP layout for Brasilian Air Force
V744	Dart RDa 3 Mk 506	Capital Airlines
V745	Dart RDa 3 Mk 506/ RDa 6 Mk 510	Capital Airlines (first nine of order)
V745D	Dart RDa 6 Mk 510	Capital Airlines (remainder of order)

Type number	Engines	Remarks
V747	Dart RDa 3 Mk 506	Butler Air Transport
V748D	Dart RDa 6 Mk 510	Central African Airways
V749	Dart RDa 3 Mk 506	LAV-Linea Aeropostal Venezolana
V754D	Dart RDa 6 Mk 510	Middle East Airlines
V755D	Dart RDa 6 Mk 510	Airwork/Cubana
V756D	Dart RDa 6 Mk 510	Trans-Australia Airlines
V757	Dart RDa 3 Mk 506	Trans-Canada Airlines
V759D	Dart RDa 6 Mk 510	Hunting-Clan
V760D	Dart RDa 6 Mk 510	Hong Kong Airways
V761D	Dart RDa 6 Mk 510	Union of Burma Airways
V763D	Dart RDa 6 Mk 510	TACA-Transportes Aéreos Centro Americanos
V764D	Dart RDa 6 Mk 510	US Steel Corporation
V765D	Dart RDa 6 Mk 510	Standard Oil Corporation
V768D	Dart RDa 6 Mk 510	Indian Airlines
V769D	Dart RDa 6 Mk 510	Pluna
V772	Dart RDa 3 Mk 506	British West Indian Airways
V773	Dart RDa 3 Mk 506	Iraqi Airways
V776D	Dart RDa 6 Mk 510	Kuwait Oil Co
V779D	Dart RDa 6 Mk 510	Fred Olsen
V781D	Dart RDa 6 Mk 510	VIP layout for South African Air Force

Below:
After serving both Capital and United in the 1950s and 1960s, N7422 was flown to Santa Barbara and broken up in 1973.
Sherlock Via G. W. Pennick

Type number	Engines	Remarks
V782D	Dart RDa 6 Mk 510	Iranian Airlines
V784D	Dart RDa 6 Mk 510	Philippine Airlines
V785D	Dart RDa 6 Mk 510	Alitalia
V789D	Dart RDa 6 Mk 510	VIP layout for Brasilian Air Force
V793D	Dart RDa 6 Mk 510	VIP layout for Royal Bank of Canada
V794D	Dart RDa 6 Mk 510	Turkish Airlines
V797D	Dart RDa 6 Mk 510	Canadian Government
V798D	Dart RDa 6 Mk 510	Northeast Airlines
V801	Dart RDa 6 Mk 510	BEA. Not built, superseded by V802
V802	Dart RDa 6 Mk 510	BEA
V803	Dart RDa 6 Mk 510	KLM

Above:
Vickers used this V745D as a demonstrator registered G-APBH in the late 1950s. It was then converted into a V798D for Northeast.
Armstrong via G. W. Pennick

Below:
A V749 for Linea Aeropostal Venezolana nears completion at Hurn in 1956. Registered YV-C-AMV, it served until 1971 when it crashed in the Andes. *Via M. J. Hooks*

Type number	Engines	Remarks
√804	Dart RDa 6 Mk 510	Transair
√805	Dart RDa 6 Mk 510	Eagle Aviation
√806	Dart RDa 7 Mk 520	BEA
√807	Dart RDa 7 Mk 520	New Zealand National Airways
√808	Dart RDa 7 Mk 520	Aer Lingus
√808C	Dart RDa 7 Mk 520	Aer Lingus freight conversion
√810	Dart RDa 7/1 Mk 525	Vickers' Series 810 prototype
√812	Dart RDa 7/1 Mk 525	Continental Airlines
√813	Dart RDa 7/1 Mk 525/530	South African Airways
√814	Dart RDa 7/1 Mk 530	Lufthansa
√815	Dart RDa 7/1 Mk 525/530	Pakistan International
√816	Dart RDa 7/1 Mk 525	Trans-Australia Airlines
√818	Dart RDa 7/1 Mk 525	Cubana
√827	Dart RDa 7/1 Mk 525	VASP
√828	Dart RDa 7/1 Mk 525	All Nippon Airways
√831	Dart RDa 7/1 Mk 525	Airwork/Sudan Airways
√832	Dart RDa 7/1 Mk 525	Ansett
√833	Dart RDa 7/1 Mk 530	Hunting-Clan
√835	Dart RDa 7/1 Mk 525	VIP layout for Tennessee Gas Transmission
√836	Dart RDa 7/1 Mk 525	VIP layout for Union Carbide Corporation
√837	Dart RDa 7/1 Mk 525	Austrian Airlines
√838	Dart RDa 7/1 Mk 525	Ghana Airways
√839	Dart RDa 7/1 Mk 525	VIP layout for Iranian Government and Union Carbide Corporation
√843	Dart RDa 7/1 Mk 525	CAAC

Below:
Built at Weybridge, the V804 was used by Transair for long distance charter work before passing through a number of hands around the world. Currently it is G-CSZB with British Air Ferries.
Via D. M. Stroud

Above:
A Viscount 806 (G-AOYR) seen in BEA's 1960s livery. In the background is D-ANIP, a Type 814 of Lufthansa.
G. W. Pennick

Right:
BAF has converted its V806 G-BLOA into a dedicated cargo carrier. It carries the name Jock Bryce OBE in honour of the pilot responsible for much of the Viscount's flight trials. *BAF*

Right:
BAF acquired G-AOYJ in April 1981 for passenger work. Later reregistered G-BLOA, it spent a time with both Manx and Guernsey Airlines before conversion to a dedicated freighter. *BAF*

Above:
When used for freight work, the seats were removed but the cabin wall lining and overhead fittings remain in place. *BAF*

Right:
The interiors of G-BBDK and G-BLOA have been completely stripped out for their freighter role. Screens protect the windows and the cargo is lashed to the floor mountings. *BAF*

Right:
Both freighters have large forward cargo doors so fairly bulky items can be loaded. *BAF*

Top left:
**Freighter G-BBDK seen before it adopted an
unpainted finish.** *BAF*

Below:
**Cubana acquired this V818 in 1959 as CU-T622.
Three years later it was sold to TAA.** *Via M. J. Hooks*

Bottom left:
**South African Airways successfully used the V810
series for some years. The pair depicted later
became G-AZLR and 'ZLT with British Midland.**
Via M. J Hooks

Bottom right:
**Used throughout as a corporate machine, the
V835 was first operated by the Tennessee Gas
Transmission Corp as N500T.**
L. Smalley via G. W. Pennick

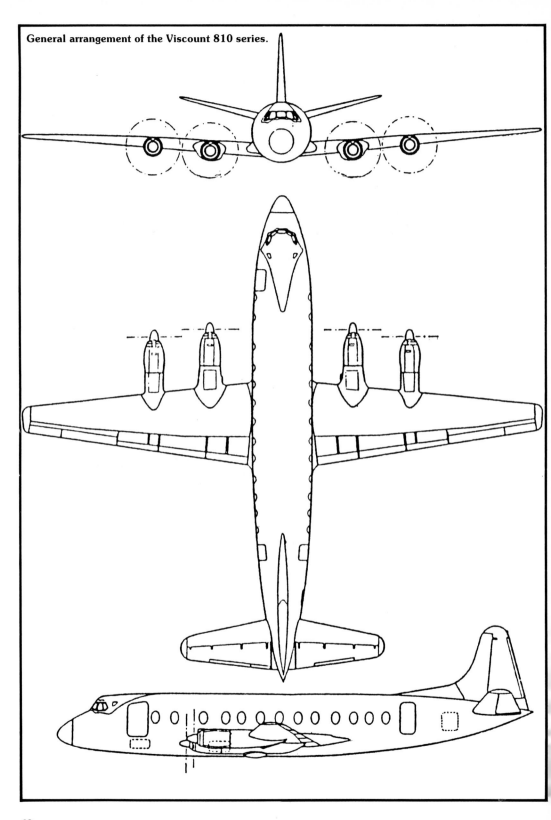

General arrangement of the Viscount 810 series.

Projects

By 1959 there were distinct signs that the Viscount's market was steadily declining, as airlines turned their attention towards the short/medium range jet types. Nevertheless, Vickers was still working on developed versions of its most successful product, aiming especially at the smaller carriers still obliged to remain faithful to the DC-3 for economic reasons.

The result of this design work was revealed on 30 January 1958 when the manufacturer announced that it could offer a Viscount tailored to the needs of local service operators. Designated Type 790, the aircraft was designed to withstand the rigours of constantly flying at low altitudes on sectors less than 500 miles. It was also expected to be of interest to carriers already flying feeder services for trunk routes, because the demand for such connections was already growing rapidly and aircraft with a larger capacity would soon be vital.

Essentially the 790 was a Series 700 incorporating a number of appropriate modifications. Most of these involved the structural changes already developed for the later Viscounts, which permitted higher landing weights and faster cruising speeds at low altitudes. Increased seating was achieved by redesigning the interior, so that the different models on offer could accommodate from between 54 and 65 passengers. The standard version of the 790 was intended to carry 13 rows of four-abreast seats at a 34in pitch, with a rear freight hold immediately forward of the aft pressure bulkhead. As an alternative, lounge-type seating could be arranged for the rear cabin which provided a total capacity for 60

passengers while retaining the same layout. However, if a five-abreast arrangement was chosen, then the numbers increased to 59 and 65 repectively. In all cases space was saved by reducing the toilet facilities to a single unit, while the galley was removed completely. These sacrifices were not considered unreasonable and should not have caused much hardship between stops.

When employed on the type of duties envisaged for the aircraft, it was desirable to fly a number of sectors before refuelling and without the need for frequent ground servicing. Quick turn-rounds were also necessary, otherwise the advantages of air travel over short distances would be lost. It could even be faster by road. Since the flights would be at a lower altitude, cabin pressurisation was reduced to 4.5psi instead of the normal 6psi. More weight saving was therefore achieved because the services of only one blower were needed. During the short pauses at intermediate stops, it was arranged that the No 4 engine would not normally be shut down, so that electrical power was available to restart the other three. Vickers chose the Dart RDa 3 Mk 506

Below:
Top: A typical V700 arrangement for 48 passengers.
Middle: A layout for a BEA V802 equipped with 53 seats.
Bottom: The 810 series had the rear four-seat lounge area in the rear, the option of an eight-seat forward cabin and the main accommodation for 44 passengers.

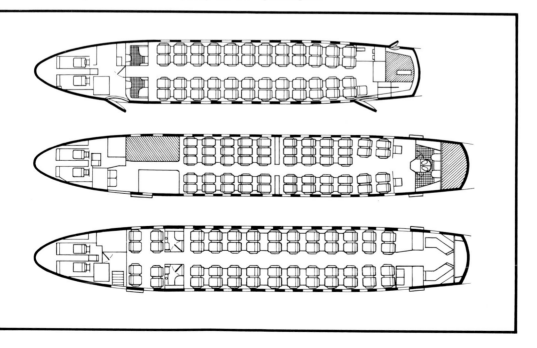

for the 790's powerplant in preference to later marks because of the background of experience and the fact that it was lighter and cheaper. Airstairs were installed as standard at the forward entrance to eliminate the danger of pushing mobile ground steps into the windmilling port propellers. While this action would have undoubtedly have stopped the movement, it was somewhat drastic. A more gentle method was adopted by fitting brakes on both port-side fans, while the No 3 propeller was similarly modified to allow fast access to the starboard freight hold without risk of injury.

Of course, the 790 was not a new design by any means, but a modified aircraft intended for a specific role. It meant that most of the various elements were already in production, so an early initial delivery date in mid-1959 was offered. For the same reason, the price of the aircraft was set at a lower level than other Viscounts, with estimated figures showing that seat-mile costs were likely to be some 10% less than those of the DC-3 even over very short stages. Yet despite some intensive marketing, particularly in the US where there were plenty of potential clients, the considerable amount of time-consuming effort remained fruitless. It was probably still too early for the small carriers to contemplate discarding their faithful piston-engined twins for a sophisticated turboprop. This view was undoubtedly justified, because even many years later the transition often remained too great a hurdle for those more ambitious than cautious.

There was more interest shown in the V840 when it was first mooted. Once again it was the prospect of the more powerful Dart RDa 11 Mk 541 which made the idea for a 400mph Viscount perfectly feasible. Since the V810 had the built-in strength to cope with the new engine, it was a relatively simple matter to convert the variant to the latest specification. Vickers received an encouraging response to its proposal, which even prompted BEA to take an option of 12 aircraft. In the event this was not taken up and no V840s were ever built, neither were any 810s converted. The Viscount's main-line domination was nearing an end and new developments were not really required by the smaller independents.

There were still two other projects on the Vickers' drawing boards, namely the V850 and V870. The former was basically similar to the 840 variant but equipped with Dart RDa 8s and known as the Viscount Major. More radical changes were introduced with the V870 including the possible use of turbojets. Vickers managed to attract the interest of both BEA and TCA, but after many discussions and changes, the 870 finally emerged as a second-generation turboprop airliner in the guise of the Vanguard. Sadly, it did not enjoy the same success as its forebear, only 43 specimens being sold. It is quite possible that had the Viscount actually become a 100-seat airliner in the 400mph class as planned, it would have brought greater fortunes to the manufacturer.

Specifications

	V630	V700
Span:	89ft 0in (27.12m)	93ft 8½in (28.56m)
Length:	74ft 6in (22.70m)	81ft 2in (24.77m)
Height:	26ft 3in (8.00m)	26ft 9in (8.15m)
Max take-off weight:	45,000lb (20,412kg)	60,000lb (27,220kg)
Max cruising speed:	300mph	318mph (Dart 505), 324mph (Dart 506)
Accommodation (seats):	32	40-53 standard. Conversions to 60-63 and 71

	V700D	V800
Span:	93ft 8 1/2in (28.56m)	93ft 8½in (28.56m)
Length:	81ft 10in (24.91m)	85ft 6in (26.06m)
Height:	26ft 9in (8.15m)	26ft 9in (8.15m)
Max take-off weight:	64,500lb (29,257kg)	64,500lb (29,257kg)
Max cruising speed:	334mph	335mph (806)
Accommodation:	40-53	53-65 standard. Conversions to 66-71

	V810
Span:	93ft 8½ft (28.56in)
Length:	85ft 8in (26.11m)
Height:	26ft 9in (8.15m)
Max take-off weight:	72,500lb (32,886kg)
Max cruising speed:	365mph
Accommodation:	56-64 standard. Conversions to 80

Seating arrangements were changed by operators as required within the limits quoted.

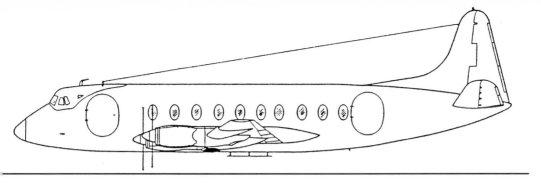

Mishaps

In the past 40 years or so, over 25% of the 444 Viscounts built have ended their days prematurely following some form of accident. A number of these were due to the inexperience of the crews, especially when attempting asymmetric take-offs, while incorrect altimeter settings also added to the fatal errors. There were relatively few caused by airframe or engine problems; flap failures being notable exceptions. Nevertheless, there were a significant number of incidents for which the cause was never revealed, the only clue being reports of 'pieces falling from the aircraft before it dived into the sea'.

Technological advances in the immediate post-war years meant that designers had little previous experience when creating a new product. It was a pioneering era, with many of the lessons learnt after aircraft had entered service, but at least the sacrifice of the few meant greater safety for the many that followed. When the Viscount first appeared it was regarded with considerable respect by older pilots converting from piston-engined twins. Manuals specified precise speeds for a multitude of situations, all to be strictly followed to the nearest knot. Unlike the present day, only rudimentary simulators

were available which meant that crew training was carried out around the circuit, a pastime that could prove risky. This was clearly demonstrated by a Trans-Australia Airlines' machine in October 1954, when it had the doubtful distinction of becoming the first Viscount to be the cause of casualties.

The V720 VH-TVA had made its maiden flight on 29 August 1954 and subsequently appeared at the SBAC Show a few days later. Once this event had ended, the aircraft was given its pre-delivery checks and formally handed over to its proud owner on 5 October. Only three weeks or so later it crashed while in use for crew training at Mangalore, Victoria. At the time the pilot under test was attempting a three-engine take-off with No 4 Dart stopped and its propeller feathered. In this configuration and with full power applied, it was not possible to prevent the Viscount from turning

Below:
Trans-Australia took delivery of VH-TVA at the beginning of October 1954, but by the end of the month it had been destroyed. *Via M. J. Hooks*

without use of its nose-wheel steering at speeds below 96kt. In order to obtain the full effect, it was therefore necessary to keep the wheel firmly on the ground until the safety speed of 106kt had been reached. On this occasion the aircraft left the runway at between 85kt and 90kt at which point it was beginning to swing badly. To correct the situation, the training captain took over the controls, but his decision to continue the flight proved disastrous. Some 2,000ft from the start of the roll, the Viscount turned through 90° before crashing into some trees to end the short career of TAA's first V720. Three of the airline's pilots were killed, but five occupants in the passenger cabin escaped with minor injuries. The ensuing investigation concluded that an error of judgement by the captain had been responsible.

Bad visibility was to blame for the take-off crash by the BEA Viscount 701, G-AMOK. Such were the conditions at Heathrow on the morning of 16 January 1955 that the aircraft's 10.00hr departure to Rome, Athens and Istanbul had been delayed. After a slight improvement in the weather, Oscar Kilo was eventually cleared to taxi along No 1 runway (now known as 27R) to the holding point of No 6 (15R). Unfortunately, due to the poor light the aircraft was turned on to the disused No 3 and take-off began. This runway had been closed for some years by this time and a solid structure now stood in the path of the accelerating airliner, namely the new centre terminal and control tower. Luckily the contractors also found the strip useful for parking stores and other impedimenta, so it was this traditionally untidy heap that Oscar Kilo first encountered. Travelling at some 70mph, the aircraft hit the objects, ploughing through a steel barrier, huts and a pile of cast iron before coming to rest. In the process the Viscount shed its undercarriage, the two port engines and suffered ruptured fuel tanks. Miraculously there was no fire and only two people were injured: the captain and one passenger. Had the aircraft become airborne, then of course it would have inevitably collided with the buildings with disastrous consequences. It was also fortuitous that it was a Sunday with few construction staff in evidence. In due course Oscar Kilo was rebuilt by Marshalls at Cambridge, returning to BEA service in 1958 with a high-density 60-seat layout, airstairs and two-crew flightdeck. The aircraft was redesignated V701X on completion.

Although 'MOK was severely bent, it did at least survive its ordeal; a fate not enjoyed by its near relative, G-AMOM, on 20 January 1956. The aircraft was being used for a crew-training detail at Blackbushe when it suffered an accident during an asymmetric take-off. With the No 4 propeller feathered for practice purposes, a problem then developed with No 3 engine during the run along the runway, encouraging the machine to swing violently to starboard. The situation was reminiscent of the Australian crash 18 months or so earlier, but in this case the training captain opted to put the wandering machine back on the ground. This sudden encounter ended the Viscount's further airborne progress and also any expectations of longevity, but at least the crew survived with only minor injuries. It was the first of the type to be lost by the Corporation since services started in April 1953.

An unwelcome statistic was also recorded by TCA on 9 July 1956 when one of its fleet was responsible for the Viscount's first passenger fatality. On this occasion the aircraft was on a flight between Chicago and Toronto when it suffered the loss of the starboard outer propeller. A part entered the fuselage causing one death and injuries to five other occupants in the cabin. Flying debris also damaged the inner engine, but the resultant fire was immediately extinguished. At the time of the incident the airliner was cruising at 18,000ft, but after an emergency descent using the two port engines, a successful landing was made at Windsor, Ontario.

Obviously it was a regrettable accident, but the operator and manufacturer were at least able to take comfort in the fact that matters could have been much worse. When the pressurised cabin was punctured, there was no further structural failure as might have been the case. In addition, the engine fire was speedily and effectively handled, while the aircraft demonstrated its ability to survive after the loss of half its power. Finally, the skill of the pilots in maintaining control throughout the crisis was not overlooked.

On 14 March 1957 BEA lost the V701 flagship G-ALWE when it crashed near Manchester (Ringway) with the loss of 15 passengers, the crew of five and a woman and child on the ground. The aircraft was making a normal approach to Runway 24 in reasonable weather conditions, when it suddenly banked to starboard as it descended. After the wingtip touched the grass about 300yd to the right of the centre line, the Viscount then hit the ground before continuing into a housing estate, whereupon fire immediately broke out.

This was the type's first crash that involved passenger fatalities in some 500,000hr of flying by more than 180 aircraft. In fact, BEA was responsible for a considerable proportion of these totals having flown 150,000hr with nearly two million passengers. Investigators quickly identified the cause of the tragedy as failure of a bolt and fitting which formed part of the support for the two inner starboard flap sections. This damage was responsible for the unexpected bank, a manoeuvre which could normally have been corrected by the use of the aileron. Unfortunately, the latter control had been locked by the failed flap giving the crew no chance to avert disaster.

During its four years in service, Whisky Echo had inaugurated a number of new routes for BEA, in

Above:
Seen on the Hurn line in 1956, N7437 was a 745D for Capital which was lost in 1958. *Via D. M. Stroud*

he process often setting a record for the particular ector. At the time of the crash it had only spent 5,900hr in the air and made 3,450 landings. Following the accident, all V700s were withdrawn for inspection and the replacement of the suspect bolts. Of the 845 examined from 100 aircraft, 33 examples produced evidence of fatigue, albeit to a minor degree. Asymmetric flaps were deemed to have caused several other mishaps in later years, including the crash at Liverpool of Cambrian's V701 G-AMOL on 20 July 1965.

Some accidents remained a mystery despite exhaustive investigations, one in this category being the incident in which the first production V802 was lost. After only a few months in service, G-AOJA crashed in poor weather while making a GCA approach to Nutts Corner, Belfast on 23 October 1957. The aircraft was on a special charter flight to pick up the Minister of Supply and a party of journalists who were visiting Short & Harland's works. Although the captain had considered diverting to Dublin or Aldergrove, he was advised that an approach could probably be made without going below the airline's minima. However, when less than a mile from touchdown the Viscount was well to the right of the centre-line, so an overshoot was initiated. A very short time later the aircraft crashed within the airport boundary with undercarriage and flaps retracted and engines at the appropriate power setting. No airframe or engine malfunction could be blamed, neither was there any evidence that pilot error contributed to the accident in which the crew of five and two passengers were killed.

BEA suffered another V802 loss on 17 November, this time involving G-AOHP which crash-landed in a field near Hellerup, 25 miles northwest of Copenhagen. The Viscount was operating a scheduled night freight service from London when it experienced an almost total loss of power. Fortunately the two-man crew was uninjured, but the aircraft was damaged beyond repair.

Across the Atlantic, Capital's first fatal crash came on the night of 6 April 1958. The V745D N7437 was operating the Newark-Detroit-Flint-Saginaw (Tri-City)-Chicago service when it came down some 2,300ft (701m) short of the runway as it approached Tri-City airport. When the CAB report was published it found that the most probable cause of the disaster was that the aircraft stalled while executing a steep turn, with the resultant spin occurring at too low an altitude for any chance of recovery. It was also thought that the situation was not improved by an inoperative stall-warning device, the presence of ice and the rather gusty conditions prevailing at the time of the accident, which was responsible for the death of all of the 44 passengers and crew of three.

65

Just over a month later Capital lost N7410 when it was in collision with an Air National Guard T-33A on 20 May. Only seven passengers were on board the airliner at the time, but they and the crew of four were killed. The same fate befell the passenger in the military trainer, but the pilot escaped by parachute despite being seriously injured. He was subsequently held responsible for the incident because of his failure 'to exercise proper and adequate vigilance to see and avoid other traffic'.

The misreading of the altimeter was blamed for the accident to the BEA Viscount 802 G-AORC on 28 April. The aircraft was positioning from Heathrow to Prestwick with a crew of five on board to pick up 24 passengers for BOAC. During the approach into the Scottish airport the captain was controlling the descent while monitoring his instruments, dealing with the RT messages, copying the weather reports, briefing the first officer on possible overshoot procedures and checking the altimeters. These were of the three needle type, an instrument not renowned for its clarity and one which could easily be misread, as in this instance. Somewhat lower than intended, Romeo Charley struck some electricity power cables before crashing into Hill of Barnwell, Craigie, some 4½ miles east-northeast of the airport. Fortunately all five of the crew not only survived the unexpected and premature landing, but also escaped from the airliner before it was consumed by fire.

A similar misinterpretation of the altimeter's reading by the pilot was thought to have been the probable reason for a crash at Benghazi, Libya on 9 August. The Central African Airways Viscount VP-YNE was operating the Zambesi service from Salisbury to London and was at the end of the sector from Wadi Halfa. There was nothing unusual about its progress as the aircraft made a direct approach to Runway 33R, but suddenly it flew into high ground and caught fire some 5½ miles from Benina airport. At the point of impact the V748D should have been at 1,650ft but in reality it hit the ground at 539ft. No defects were found in the aircraft or its equipment, which led to the conclusion that the height had been misread by the crew. Remarkably, there were 18 survivors from the crash, but sadly another 36 died including the pilots and cabin staff.

Mid-air collisions are fortunately rare, but in its career the Viscount has unluckily been involved in more than its fair share of encounters. The victim in another 1958 incident was BEA's G-ANHC, a V701 flying from London to Malta via Naples with a normal scheduled service on 22 October. At 23,500ft above Anzio, the aircraft unexpectedly met an Italian Air Force F-86 with disastrous consequences. All 26 passengers and five crew were killed but the fighter pilot managed to survive the ordeal. Over two years earlier in June 1956, the airliner had

been the first of its type to carry HM The Queen and other members of the Royal Family.

Cuba has always been a haven for hijackers and on 1 November Cubana's V755 CU-T603 was the target for a five-man group while operating the airline's flight 495 from Miami to Varadero. While en route, the rebels produced uniforms and machine guns and instructed the captain to change course. After refusing to co-operate, he was forcibly removed from the controls which were then taken over by one of the bandits. Obviously the individual had some knowledge of flying because he turned the aircraft to head towards a landing area in Oriente Province, near to Castro's guerrilla stronghold in the mountains. Landing was not quite so easy, especially since it was getting dark and the strip was unlit. By this time, the Viscount's fuel state was becoming critical, a fact probably overlooked by the pseudo pilot. Finally the doomed airliner landed in the sea off the Cuban coast, whereupon 17 of the 20 occupants lost their lives unnecessarily. The event was duly recorded as being the first known hijack to cause the death of innocent passengers.

Ten days later, on 10 November, a V724 (CF-TGL) of TCA had the misfortune to be attacked by Super Constellation N6503C at Idlewild (later JFK), New York. The latter aircraft managed to ignite both itself and the Viscount in the course of the ground confrontation, inflicting sufficient damage for the pair to be declared write-offs. Only the respective crews were on board at the time and there were no casualties. There was a similar outcome after two other ground collisions involving Viscounts.

On 2 December one of Hunting-Clan's V732s (G-ANRR) took-off from Heathrow on a post-overhaul test flight. Almost immediately it was apparent that the machine was experiencing trouble, a fact confirmed by the radio messages received during the 14min it remained in the air. During this time it was virtually impossible to maintain a straight and level attitude due to the violent, uncontrolled movements, which continued until the machine finally broke up near Camberley. Amongst the six members of the flight and engineering crew was Hunting's chief pilot, Capt R. W. L. Mulliner DFC, who had joined the company in 1946. This sad loss resulted from the incorrect reassembly of an elevator spring-tab, thereby effectively reversing its operation. Apparently new parts intended for the starboard elevator had been fitted in error to the corresponding control on the opposite side.

After a very gloomy 1958 indeed it was to be hoped that the New Year would produce fewer accidents, but on 17 February 1959 a Viscount 794 (TC-SEV) belonging to Turkish Airlines crashed near Gatwick. The six-month old aircraft was carrying the country's Prime Minister and his staff for the signing of the tripartite treaty on Cyprus, so it was a particularly delicate situation. The flight had routed via Rome on its journey from Istanbul with the intention of landing at Heathrow, but conditions necessitated its diversion. Its approach into Gatwick appeared quite normal, but it hit the ground in Jordan's Wood, near Rusper, some 3½ miles west of the airport. At this point the aircraft should have been at about 1,000ft in relation to the runway, so it was assumed that the altimeter had been incorrectly set or read. Of the 25 occupants, 10 survived, including the Prime Minister.

Continental had two major accidents with its V812s during the eight years or so that the type was operated by the airline. The first of these occurred on 8 July 1962 when N243V was written off at Amarillo Municipal, Tx. There were 13 passengers and three crew on the aircraft as it lifted-off the runway at the start of a normal scheduled service, but with undercarriage retracted, the machine sank back on to the ground. Although the resultant fire destroyed the airliner, miraculously everyone survived. In the absence of any defects being discovered by the investigating team, the latter decided that the most likely cause was that the captain had allowed the aircraft to wander after being distracted by some water dripping on to his arm.

There were fatalities in Continental's second Viscount crash which happened as N242V approached Kansas Municipal on 28 January 1963. After lowering the flaps, a 3in accumulation of ice on the tail caused the nose to drop virtually out of control. Subsequently the V812 overran the runway prior to hitting a high river embankment and being destroyed by fire. The crew of four were among the nine killed by the accident.

Of the surviving 812s sold to Channel Airways in 1967, two were destroyed at Southend. The first was G-AVJZ which, as N248V, had been delivered on 15 April. With its overhaul complete, the aircraft took-off on 3 May for a routine C of A test flight. Soon after it had left the runway, the Viscount suddenly banked to starboard until the wingtip hit the ground, spinning the aircraft round to crash in flames at one end of the airport's scrapyard. Before coming to rest it struck a crane and demolished a wooden hut, killing two of the three local workers inside. Once again a simulated engine-out test was underway, the familiar No 4 being the shut-down powerplant.

Almost exactly one year later Channel suffered another Viscount crash at Southend. On the evening of 4 May 1968, the V812 G-APPU landed on Runway 06 in heavy rain only to aquaplane it way off the end. It struck the adjacent railway embankment at an angle before sliding up the grass bank, in so doing distributing sections of its undercarriage around the area. This action complete, the fuselage split open as it came to rest at the top of the mound, but as a final gesture an engine detached itself to block the Southend-Liverpool Street main line for several hours. Incredibly there was no fire despite considerable quantities of fuel flowing from the split tanks. It was equally amazing that there were no fatalities, although several passengers were detained in hospital under observation. Maybe 'PPU was attempting to become the first Skytrain, but neither the airline nor BR was impressed. Within a few days the remains had been cut up and the pieces removed by lorry.

On the last day of the year the V720 VH-RMC suffered a particularly unpleasant accident while on a flight from Perth, Australia. One of the original batch delivered to Trans-Australia as VH-TVB, the machine was subsequently sold to Ansett-ANA and later leased to MacRobertson-Miller in September 1968. Three months later a structural failure of the wing caused the aircraft to break up with the loss of the five crew and 25 passengers. As a result of this disaster, all Viscount 700s were grounded in Australia pending an investigation into the cause. In due course the ban was lifted on the V756Ds but remained in force for both V720s and V747s.

A decidedly unorthodox landing was made by the oldest airworthy surviving Viscount on 17 July 1980. Earlier that day G-ARBY had left Exeter with a full fuel load on an IT flight to Santander, Spain which was reached uneventfully. During the course of the turn-round, the tanks were fully topped-up which should have provided more than adequate fuel for the return leg. This did not prove the case because some miles short of its UK destination, the Viscount was suddenly transformed into a glider. As a consequence of some impressive handling by the Captain, a safe forced landing was made in a field at Bishops Court Farm, Ottery St Mary, six miles from Exeter. There were no serious casualties amongst the 62 people on board, but of course the aircraft's flying days were over. After a lengthy investigation into the mishap, it was decided that most of the blame rested with the crew for failing to carry out the physical 'dip-stick' check on the tank contents at Santander. However, the committee was also convinced, but could not prove, that the Spanish bowser had pumped far less fuel into the Viscount than the flowmeters had indicated.

Despite these sobering events, of which only a representative sample have been included, the Viscount has given superb service to the travelling public for four decades with no loss of popularity, a record difficult to achieve and even harder to retain.

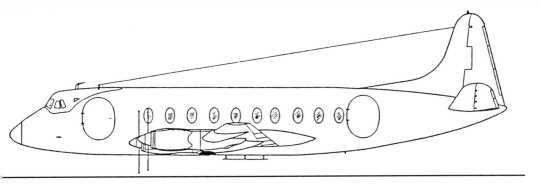

Operators

Although Vickers sold new Viscounts to some 60 operators, the latter increased considerably in numbers once secondhand examples of the type became available. Many are listed in this section, but aircraft operated on short leases are not included. Similarly the aircraft were not necessarily in the airlines' fleets at the same time. Brief details of the individual machines used contain type, constructor's number and registration.

Aden Airways
Both aircraft were acquired secondhand in 1963 for use on the airlines regional services. A bomb destroyed 'AAW while on the ground at Aden in June 1967.
V760D: 186/7 (VR-AAV/W)

Aer Lingus
The Irish flag carrier was amongst the first to order the V700 series with deliveries starting in March 1954. First commercial service was on the Dublin-Manchester-Brussels-Frankfurt route on 15 April using EI-AFV. The company later ordered the V800 in two batches but doubled its fleet by acquiring KLM's V803s in 1966.
V707: 30-32/4 (EI-AFV/W, Y, AGI) **V803:** 172-80 (EI-AOG/OJ/PD/OL/OF/OE/OM/OI/OH). **V808:** 258 (EI-AMA), 289-91 (EI-AJI-K), 312 (EI-ALG), 421/3 (EI-AKO, KK/L)

Below:
The Viscount 808 EI-AKL was one of an order placed by Aer Lingus. *AJW*

Above:
Aer Lingus bought the entire KLM fleet of Viscounts in 1966, often leasing them out, as in the case of EI-AOI with BAF in 1970. *AJW*

Aerolineas Condor

The Viscount was intended for the company's scheduled domestic routes in Ecuador but was soon seriously damaged.
V745D: 205 (HC-BHB)

Aerolineas TAO

Alitalia was the source of the three Viscounts, all of which suffered mishaps in the hands of the Colombian operator ranging from wheels-up landings to encounters with mountains.
V745D: 118 (HK-1057). **V785D:** 327 (HK-1061), 380 (HK-1058)

Aeropesca Colombia

This airline acquired its Viscounts in the 1970s for use on its considerable domestic and international network. In 1983 its name was changed to Intercontinental de Aviacion, but its use of the British turboprop airliners continued into the 1990s.
V745D: 112 (HK-1320), 138 (HK-1708), 212 (HK-1773/2382). **V798D:** 232 (HK-1319)

Aerovias del Cesar

See Transportes Aereos del Cesar

Air Botswana

The airline introduced the Viscount on to its scheduled service to Johannesburg in 1977.
V754D: 243 (A2-ABD). **V761D:** 189 (A2-ABY)

Air Canada

See Trans-Canada Airlines.

Air Commerz

This Hamburg-based airline was formed in 1970 with a pair of Viscounts to operate IT charters. After two years the company became bankrupt whereupon the aircraft were repossessed by Aer Lingus.
V808: 421/3 (D-ADAN/M)

Below:
Air Canada inherited a number of Viscounts from TCA including CF-TGK. *Via M. J. Hooks*

71

Right:
Air France ordered 12 Viscount 708s; F-BGNV joining the fleet in 1954. It crashed in 1963 while serving with Air Inter. *AJW*

Below right:
The French domestic carrier, Air Inter, acquired the V708 from Starways in 1963, re-registering it as F-BLHI. Later it returned to the UK to serve with a number of airlines. *G. W. Pennick*

Air Ferry
Two V812s were leased from Channel Airways at the beginning of 1968 to operate IT charters from Manston, Newcastle, Gatwick and Manchester. At the end of the first summer season Air Ferry ceased operations and returned the two Viscounts to Channel.
V812: 361 (G-AVNJ), 363 (G-AVHE)

Air France
The French flag carrier became the first foreign operator of the Viscount after ordering 12 V708s in November 1951. Services began on 15 September 1953 on the London-Paris route.
V708: 8 (F-BGNK), 10 (F-BGNL), 12 (F-BGNM), 14 (F-BGNN), 16 (F-BGNO), 18 (F-BGNP), 33 (F-BGNQ), 35 (F-BGNR), 36 (F-BGNS), 37 (F-BGNT), 38 (F-BGNU), 39 (F-BGNV)

Air Inter
When Air France began to withdraw its Viscounts in the early 1960s, the French domestic carrier took delivery of the survivors for use on its own services. Later four ex-Canadian V724s were also purchased.
V708: 10 (F-BOEC), 12 (F-BOEA), 14 (F-BOEB), 16 (F-BGNO), 18 (F-BGNP), 33 (F-BGNQ), 35 (F-BGNR), 36 (F-BLHI), 37 (F-BGNT), 38 (F-BGNU), 39 (F-BGNV). **V724:** 50 (F-BMCH), 52 (F-BMCG), 54 (F-BMCF), 55 (F-BNAX)

Air International
After taking delivery of a V702 in July 1971, Air International marked the start of its operations with a charter flight to Frankfurt on 4 September. This type of work continued until November 1972 when the aircraft was impounded at Gatwick before returning to the lessor at East Midlands. Plans were made for a restart in 1973, but neither the company nor Viscount flew again.
V702: 73 (G-APPX)

Air Laos
Scheduled services were started in 1976, one ex-Indian Airlines Viscount being used for the domestic sectors.
V768D: 294 (RDPL-3-4016)

Air Malawi
Formed in September 1967, the airline acquired a pair of Viscounts to handle the scheduled services in the newly-created State that was previously known as Nyasaland.
V748D: 98 (7Q-YDK). **V754D:** 241 (7Q-YDL)

Air Rhodesia
See Air Zimbabwe.

Air Tourisme Alpin SA
This company was formed in 1969 to operate cargo charter flights from its base at Basle. A convertible passenger/freight Viscount was acquired from SATA in 1972 but the aircraft was repossessed by Aer Lingus in the same year.
V808: 291 (HB-ILR)

Air Ulster
For six months or so in 1969 the Belfast-based car-

Above:
The Viscount 702 G-APPX had a short career with Air International. AJW

ier leased a Viscount from Aer Lingus. During its stay the aircraft's main employment centred around the company's regular link with Prestwick, since earlier plans to use it for IT work did not materialise. Shortly after the V803 was returned to Dublin, Air Ulster was forced to cease trading due to heavy losses, no doubt much of it due to the under-utilised Viscount.

V803: 174 (EI-APD)

Airwork Ltd

During 1958 the company introduced Viscounts on to the colonial coach class service to Africa operated in association with Hunting-Clan. In June 1959 the company began the Blue Nile schedule on behalf of Sudan Airways, taking the V831s employed on this weekly task to Rome, Athens and Cairo en route to Khartoum. In 1960 Airwork merged with Hunting-Clan and Air Charter to create British United, whereupon the Viscounts were given the new titles and livery.

V736: 77/8 (G-AODG/H). **V831:** 402/3 (G-APND/E)

Air Zimbabwe

The airline was formed in September 1967 as Air Rhodesia after the dissolution of Central African Airways. Services to neighbouring countries were flown by a fleet of Viscounts, which then remained in the fleet until the late 1980s. In 1980 the carrier adopted the title Air Zimbabwe to coincide with the country's independence.

V748D: 98 (VP-YNA/Z-YNA), 99 (VP-YNB/Z-YNB), 100 (VP-YNC/Z-YNC). **V754D:** 240 (VP-WAR/Z-WAR), 241 (VP-YTE/VP-WJI/Z-WJI), 243 (VP-YTE/Z-YTE). **V756D:** 374 (VP-YNI/Z-YNI). **V782D:** 297 (VP-WAS), 298 (VP-WAT/Z-WAT). **V838:** 436 (VP-WGB/Z-WGB). **V839:** 446 (VP-WGC/Z-WGC)

Alia-Royal Jordanian Airline

See Jordanian Airways.

Alidair

The company purchased the few remaining serviceable V812s after the collapse of Channel Airways in 1972. An ex-British Midland machine was then added to the fleet allowing charter operations to begin from East Midlands. During the next couple of years this activity was expanded to include day trips to Holland from a number of airports, while in Scotland oil-related flights were commonplace. A shortage of capacity in 1975 brought several ex-Air Inter V708s into the fleet, which were ideal for the northern operations. In 1977 Guernsey Airlines became a subsidiary company using a Viscount transferred from the parent. Alidair later traded as Inter City but was forced to cease operations in 1983.

V708: 10 (G-ARBY), 14 (G-ARGR), 36 (G-ARIR), 37 (G-BDIK). **V724:** 52 (G-BDRC). **V735:** 67 (G-BFMW), 69 (G-BFYZ). **V812:** 357 (G-ATUE), 358 (G-AVIW), 353 (N501TL), 389 (G-AVJL) **V814:** 342 (G-AZNH). **V831:** 419 (G-ASED)

Alidair leased its Viscounts to a number of carriers including BAF, which employed the V812 G-AVIW in 1973. *AJW*

Above:
Guernsey Airlines was a subsidiary of Alidair, the source of Viscount 724 G-BDRC. *AJW*

Alitalia
The Italian flag carrier became a Viscount operator following its merger with Linee Aeree Italiane (LAI) in 1957. Six V785Ds had been ordered by LAI, a number subsequently increased to 10. Secondhand specimens were also added to the fleet, in most cases one-time members of the Capital fleet. By the end of the 1960s Alitalia had disposed of the surviving Viscounts.
V745D: 114 (I-LIRC), 116 (I-LIRE), 118 (I-LIRT), 119 (I-LITS), 130 (I-LIFS), 131 (I-LINS). **V785D:** 325 (I-LIFE), 326 (I-LIFT), 327 (I-LILI), 328 (I-LAKE), 329 (I-LARK), 330 (I-LOTT), 377 (I-LIRS), 378 (I-LIZT), 379 (I-LIRP), 380 (I-LIZO). **V798D:** 284 (I-LIRG), 288 (I-LIRM)

All Nippon
The Japanese company ordered Viscounts for its comprehensive domestic network at a late stage in the types production, eventually taking delivery of nine of some of the last specimens built. Two additional aircraft were leased to the airline by Vickers so that crew training could proceed from mid-1960, both machines having been previously employed in a similar role by both Capital and Continental.
V744: 88/9 (G-APKJ/K). **V828:** 443-5 (JA8201-3), 448-50 (JA8205-7), 457-9 (JA8208-10)

Aloha Airlines
When Aloha introduced three Viscounts on to the frequent Hawaiian inter-island sectors it proved a very popular decision with the travellers. After a fourth example joined the fleet in 1965, the quartet maintained the schedules until 1969 when one was written-off. The survivors continued until 1971 when the new Boeing 737 took over the duties.
V745D: 112/113 (N7414/5). **V754D:** 242 (N7410). **V798D:** 232 (N7416)

Ansett-ANA
Four new V832s were ordered for 1959 delivery so that the type could takeover the company's exten-

Above:
Five of Alitalia's collection of Viscount 700s including I-LIFE, LIRS, LIFT and LIZT. *Via AJW*

sive inter-state routes in Australia. Subsequently other machines were bought or leased, the fleet at one point consisting of 12 aircraft. The type was finally withdrawn at the end of the 1960s.
V720: 45 (VH-RMQ), 46 (VH-TVC), 48/9 (VH-TVE/F). **V747:** 97 (VH-RMO), 145 (VH-RMP). **V812:** 355 (VH-RMK). **V818:** 319 (VH-RML). **V832:** 414/7 (VH-RMG/J)

Aqua-Avia Skybus

This short-lived organisation arranged to lease the V802 G-AOHT from BAF soon after the latter had taken delivery from British Airways. On 14 Septem-ber 1981 the aircraft set off on the longest journey of its career, flying via Graz, Athens, Luxor, Bahrain, Muscat, Bombay, Calcutta, Bangkok, Singapore, Denpassar, Darwin, Nouma and Auckland. The intended Skybus service failed to materialise so the Viscount returned to the UK, eventually arriving at Southend from Zagreb on 2 April 1982.
V802: 168 (G-AOHT/ZK-SKY)

Arkia

From the end of the 1960s a number of Viscounts were acquired from a variety of sources for the air-

Below:
All Nippon leased the V744 from Vickers in 1960 for crew training purposes. It retained its UK registration G-APKK. *Via M. J. Hooks*

Soon after the V802 G-AOHT was delivered, BAF found work for it with Aqua-Avia Skybus in New Zealand. Its journey hardly seemed worth the effort because within months it was back at Southend. *BAF*

Below:
Northeast operated this V798D as N6590C until sold to Aloha as N7416 in 1963. The mark had previously been used by a Capital machine several years earlier. *J. Sherlock via G. W. Pennick*

Bottom left:
Austrian Airlines leased this V779D (OE-LAE) from Fred Olsen towards the end of the 1950s. *G. W. Pennick*

Bottom right:
Aviaco's sole Viscount was EC-AZK. *G. W. Pennick*

ine's domestic scheduled services in Israel. The type was retained until the early 1980s, but a company reorganisation then hastened the disposal of he survivors.

V819: 370 (4X-AVA). **V825:** 424 (4X-AVB). **V833:** 425/6 (4X-AVC/D). **V814:** 341 (4X-AVI), 344 (4X-AVH). **V831:** 402/3 (4X-AVF/E), 419 (4X-AVG)

Austrian Airlines

The airline began operating the Viscount at the beginning of 1958 when it leased four from Fred Olsen for use on European schedules. These aircraft were released in the spring of 1960 by the delivery of the carrier's six new machines, to which were added two second-hand specimens in the following year. All had left the company by the early 1970s.

V745D: 112/3 (OE-LAN/O). **V779D:** 247 (OE-LAE), 250-2 (OE-LAB-D). **V837:** 437-9 (OE-LAF-H), 440-2 (OE-LAK/AM)

Austrian Air Transport

Formed in 1964 as a subsidiary of Austrian Airlines, the company operated two Viscounts on lease from the parent for charter flights

V837: 440 (OE-LAK), 442 (OE-IAM)

Aviaco

One Viscount was operated by the Spanish carrier for its numerous IT flights during the 1965 summer season.

V831: 419 (EC-AZK)

Bahamas Airways

A number of Viscounts were used from 1961 on the company's scheduled services linking Nassau with Miami, Fort Lauderdale and West Palm Beach. Operations were ceased on 16 October 1970 when the company became bankrupt, but by this time the aircraft had already found other homes.

V701: 13 (VP-BCH). **V702:** 71 (VP-BBW), 72 (VP-BCD), 73 (VP-BBV). 81 (VP-BCI). **V707:** 31/2 (VP-BCF/E)

Baltic Airlines

This carrier commenced operations in June 1988 with a fleet of four ex-British Midland Viscounts. It was proposed to operate *ad hoc* charters under the name Hot Air, with any future scheduled services flown by Baltic. The company shared a common ownership with the Swedish operator of the same name, but in 1989 was merged into British Air Ferries.

V813: 349 (G-BMAT/OHOT), 350 (G-AZNA). **V814:** 338 (G-BAPF), 344 (G-BAPG)

Baltic Aviation (Sweden)

A Viscount was obtained in 1985 from British Air Ferries for cargo work, but after several years of trading, the Swedish company ceased operations in 1990 and the aircraft was stored.

V815: 375 (SE-IVY)

BKS Air Transport

This independent carrier leased three Viscounts at the start of the 1961 season, mainly to operate both schedules and IT flights from Newcastle. All were returned at the end of the year, after which BKS became engaged in a lengthy battle for survival. It was not until 1966 that the Viscount reappeared in the airline's livery for use on services radiating from Leeds. The following year brought an association with British Air Services, which in due course resulted in the transfer of some of BEA's V806s to the fleet. On 1 November 1970, BKS changed its name to Northeast Airlines, at the same time repainting the Viscounts in a predominantly yellow livery. Sadly, this distinctive scheme was soon replaced by the drab British Airways' colours after the flag carrier absorbed the regional airline three years later.

V701: 13 (G-AMOC). **V702:** 71 (G-APTA). **V707:** 34 (G-APZC). **V708:** 10 (G-ARBY),12 (G-BRER), 14 (G-ARGR). **V745D:** 124 (G-ATTA). **V776D:** 225 (G-APNF). **V786D:** 333 (G-AVIY). **V798D:** 286 (G-AVED). **V806:** 261 (G-AOYL), 264 (G-AOYO), 266 (G-AOYR), 311 (G-AOYH), 381/2 (G-APEX/Y)

Botswana National Airways

The carrier acquired a Viscount in March 1969 for use on scheduled international services, but in July of the same year the company went into liquidation.

V756D: 374 (A2-ZEL)

Bouraq Indonesia Airlines

A single example was leased in March 1980, but its stay was abruptly terminated in August by a crash

Below:
Baltic operated several V810s before it merged with BAF. *BAF*

near Jakarta. In 1983 the airline acquired four Viscounts from CAAC which have subsequently been successfully employed on scheduled services in Indonesia.

V812: 353 (PK-IVS). **V843:** 451 (PK-IVZ), 452 (PK-IVW), 454 (PK-IVX), 455 (PK-IVY)

British Air Ferries

With the availability of the well maintained but inexpensive Viscounts retired by British Airways in the early 1980s, BAF turned to new ventures. Initially six aircraft were acquired, the first to arrive at Southend being the V802, G-AOHV. After a thorough refurbishment, the aircraft were quickly despatched on lease to overseas customers. The contracts obtained encouraged BAF to purchase more of the type from BA, until eventually the fleet reached 17 at one point. Throughout the 1980s the Viscounts were operated on scheduled, charter and freight work and although several of the machines have subsequently been withdrawn, a healthy number have had the life-extension modifications incor-

Top:

BAF wrapped some bands around the Viscount's basic BA livery when the aircraft were bought in the early 1980s. *AJW*

Above:

When BAF was acquired by new owners in the early 1980s, the company introduced a new livery for the Viscounts as shown by G-APEY. *AJW*

porated to keep them active into the next century. In the late 1980s the company merged with Baltic Airlines, another Viscount operator based at Southend.

V802: 161/2 (G-AOHL/M), 168 (G-AOHT), 170 (G-AOHV/G-BLNB). **V803:** 179 (EI-AOI). **V806:** 256 (G-AOYG), 257 (G-AOYI/G-LOND), 259 (G-AOYJ/G-BLOA), 261-7 (G-AOYL-S), 311 (G-AOYH/G-BNAA), 381/2 (G-APEX/Y), 412 (G-APIM). **V807:** 248 (G-CSZB). **V808C:** 291 (G-BBDK). **V812:** 358 (G-AVIW). **V813:** 349

(G-OHOT), 350 (G-AZNA). **V814:** 338/344 (G-BAPF/G). **V815:** 375 (G-AVJB). **V836:** 435 (G-BFZL)

British Air Services
Ses BKS Air Transport and Cambrian Airways.

British Airways
The carrier formally assumed ownership of the BEA, Cambrian and Northeast fleets on 1 July 1973. It then continued to operate the Viscount until the 1980s when the type was finally withdrawn after nearly 30 years service with the national carrier.
V701: 7 (G-AMOG), 27 (G-AMON). **V802:** 151-5 (G-AOJB-F), 156/7 (G-AOHG/H), 159-64 (G-AOHJ-O), 166-8 (G-AOHR-T), 170 (G-AOHV), 171 (G-AORD), 253 (G-AOHW). **V806:** 256/7 (G-AOYG/I), 259 (G-AOYJ), 261-7 (G-AOYL-S), 311 (G-AOYH), 381/2 (G-APEX/Y), 412 (G-APIM). **V814:** 341 (G-BAPE), 344 (G-BAPG)

British Caledonian Airways
Shortage of capacity in 1985 resulted in BCal leasing a Viscount from BAF as a temporary expedient. After being repainted in the airline's full livery, the aircraft spent the summer visiting Brussels and Jersey until its duties ended in October.
V806: 266 (G-AOYR)

Bottom:
Many of the British Air Service's Viscounts were broken up at the beginning of the 1970s. Here Cambrian's V701 G-AMOC prepares for the inevitable at Rhoose. *AJW*

British Eagle

Two Viscount 805s were ordered in 1957 with the first delivered at the end of the following year. One of the pair was despatched to serve with Eagle Airways (Bermuda) on routes from the island to the Caribbean and New York. The second was employed on the company's growing number of scheduled services originating from Blackbushe, Birmingham and Manchester. When the V805s were sold in 1960, the company bought two 700 series aircraft from Cubana as replacements, other examples of this version thereafter joining the airline from time to time. After taking over the Liverpool-based Starways, Eagle's domestic network grew considerably, although the company always had to battle to win licences. Three Viscounts remained in the fleet when the airline collapsed in November 1968.

V701: 5 (G-ALWF), 9 (G-AMOA), 13 (G-AMOC), 17 (G-AMOE), 21 (G-AMOH), 28 (G-AMOO). **V707:** 30 (G-APZB), 31/2 (G-ARKH/I). **V732:** 75 (G-ANRS). **V739:** 87 (G-ATDU). **V739A:** 393/4 (G-ATDR/TFN). **V755:** 92/3 (G-AOCB/C). **V805:** 258 (G-APDW), 312 (G-APDX)

British European Airways

Over 70 Viscounts were owned by the Corporation in the late 1950s, but even this total was insufficient. Therefore a number of leases were

Below:
British Eagle bought G-ANRS in 1965, thereafter using it on schedules and ITs. It is seen waiting at Newquay before returning to Heathrow.
Via M. J. Hooks

Viscount G-AOYR carried BCal's livery for one season in 1985. *AJW*

made from time to time, Fred Olsen supplying several aircraft when required. Although the remaining V701s were given high-density seating and airstairs in 1960 for use on the German internal routes, all had been sold by mid-1963. The V802s were shared between the newly-created Channel Islands and Scottish Airways divisions in 1971, so that when BEA became a part of British Airways in 1973, the type was still very much in evidence on the regional routes.

V701: 4/5 (G-ALWE/F), 6 (G-AMNY), 7 (G-AMOG), 9 (G-AMOA), 11, (G-AMOB), 13 (G-AMOC), 15 (G-AMOD), 17 (G-AMOE), 19 (G-AMOF), 21-30 (G-AMOH-P), 61-6 (G-ANHA-F), 182 (G-AOFX). **V732:** 75 (G-ANRS). **V736:** 77/8 (G-AODG/H). **V779D:** 247 (G-ARBW), 250 (G-APZP). **V802:** 150-5 (G-AOJA-F), 156-70 (G-AOHG-V), 171 (G-AORD), 253 (G-AOHW), 254 (G-AORC). **V806:** 256 (G-AOYG), 257 (G-AOYI), 259-68 (G-AOYJ-T), 381/2 (G-APEX/Y), 396 (G-APKF), 412 (G-APIM), 413 (G-APJU), 418 (G-APOX)

Left:
Fred Olsen was the source of BEA's leased V736 G-AODH in the 1950s. *AJW*

British Midland Airways

It was January 1967 when the company introduced its first Viscount, but by the middle of the year, most of the regular schedules were flown by the type. Several new routes were launched which kept the motley collection of V700s busy, but the fleet was gradually reduced as BMA entered the jet age with three One-Elevens. A change of policy in 1972 brought the entire fleet of South African Airways' V813s to East Mildands, which, together with other additional machines, then continued on the routes until 1988, albeit in declining numbers.

V702: 73 (G-APPX). **V736:** 77 (G-AODG). **V755:** 92/3 (G-AOCB/C). **V760:** 186 (G-AWCV). **V785:** 116 (G-AWGV). **V813:** 346-9 (G-AZLP-T), 350-2 (G-AZNA-C). **V814:** 338 (G-BAPF), 339 (G-AWXI), 340/1 (G-BAPD/E), 344 (G-BAPG). **V815:** 336 (G-AVJA), 375 (G-AVJB). **V831:** 402/3 (G-APND/E), 419 (G-ASED). **V833:** 426 (G-APTD)

British Overseas Airways

In a surprising move, BOAC leased a pair of V701s from Cambrian in the early 1970s to provide feeder services between Prestwick, Belfast and Edinburgh. These were operated on a daily basis with the aircraft painted in the Corporation's full livery and named *Scottish Prince* and *Scottish Princess*. When the V701's tour of duty ended, 'MOG was donated to the Cosford Museum and repainted in a BEA

Below and Below left:
Towards the end of BEA's existence it reorganised its regional activities into separate divisions, Viscount 802 G-AOHS being allocated to Scottish Airways, while G-AOHT was nominally employed by Channel Islands. *AJW*

The V814 G-BAPF was once D-ANUN with Lufthansa. It served with BMA from the mid-1970s until going to Baltic towards the end of the next decade. *AJW*

Right:
BMA operated the Viscount until 1988 by which time G-AZNA had been repainted in the current livery. *AJW*

scheme. Their place at Prestwick was taken by two British Midland series 800s in 1976/77, but by this time British Airways was the operator concerned.
V701: 7 (G-AMOG), 27 (G-AMON)

British United Airways

The airline was created in 1960 by the merger of Airwork, Hunting-Clan, Morton Air Services, Olley Air Services, Transair and Air Charter, plus Silver City in January 1962. A number of Viscounts were therefore inherited to continue working on numerous scheduled services including those to Africa. When the type was replaced on the longer sectors, it was then gainfully employed on trooping flights between the UK and Germany. During the 1960s the Viscounts also flew on many IT charters to the Mediterranean area, but by the end of 1969 all had left the BUA fleet.

V708: 10 (G-ARBY), 12 (G-ARER), 14 (G-ARGR). **V736:** 77/8 (G-AODG/H). **V804:** 248/9 (G-AOXU/V), 395 (G-APKG). **V831:** 402/3 (G-APND/E), 419 (G-ASED). **V833:** 424-6 (G-APTB-D)

British West Indian Airways

Four Viscounts were ordered in 1953 with delivery specified for 1955, thereby enabling the company to operate its first turboprop service on 2 December. Eventually eight examples were flown on routes radiating all over the Caribbean and north to New York.

V702: 71/73 (VP-TBK/M), 81 (VP-TBN/9Y-TBN). **V772:** 235 (VP-TBS/9Y-TBS), 236 (VP-TBT/9Y-TBT), 237 (VP-TBU/9Y-TBU), 238 (VP-TBX/9Y-TBX)

Butler Air Transport

A network of feeder services was flown by Butler when it ordered two Viscounts in June 1954, the first entering service in 1955. It was joined a year later by the second example and together they were

Below:
British United was operating the ex-Transair Viscount G-AODG in 1965. *G. W. Pennick*

employed upon the Australian carrier's schedules until 1958, when the company was taken over by Ansett. The two Viscounts became the first of the type to appear on the second-hand market, but in the event they were not sold.

V747: 97 (VH-BAT), 145 (VH-BUT)

CAAC

The final customer for the Viscount was the Civil Aviation Administration of China (CAAC). An order for six aircraft was placed in December 1961 to become the first for a Western-built aircraft. After delivery in 1963/1964, the aircraft remained in regular service until 1983 when two were transferred to the Chinese Air Force, while the others were sold to Bouraq Indonesian.

V843: 451 (B-402), 452 (B-404), 453 (B-406), 454 (B-408), 455 (B-410), 456 (B-412)

Californian Eastern Airlines

Vickers received an order for eight V823s from this US carrier, but the company became bankrupt before the aircraft (c/ns 404-411) could be built.

Cambrian Airways

It was 1963 when Cambrian took delivery of its first ex-BEA V701 at a time when the airline's scheduled network was expanding. Other examples of the species were obtained from Channel until the Welsh carrier had 12 in service in 1966. In the following year Cambrian joined BKS as a member of British Air Services, whereupon it became responsible for all Viscount maintenance in both fleets. Before the last of the 701s was retired in 1971, the company had received eight V806s from the BEA collection. These were given a smart orange livery before taking over the familiar routes on the west-

ern side of the UK, but unfortunately in 1972 Cambrian came under the direct control of the newly-formed British Airways. This marked the end of any ideas for an individual identity, so before long the Viscounts were repainted in the colours of the national carrier. Most of the retired V701s were scrapped, but the oldest surviving specimen (G-ALWF) was saved for preservation at Liverpool (later Duxford), while G-AMOG eventually took up permanent residence at Cosford.

V701: 5 (G-ALWF), 7 (G-AMOG), 9 (G-AMOA), 13 (G-AMOC), 17 (G-AMOE), 20 (G-AMNZ), 21 (G-AMOH), 23 (G-AMOJ), 25 (G-AMOL), 27/9 (G-AMON/P). **V806:** 256/7 (G-AOYG/H), 259 (G-AOYJ), 262/3 (G-AOYM/N), 265 (G-AOYP), 267 (G-AOYS), 412 (G-APIM)

Capital Airlines (US)

While BEA played a large part in the Viscount's success, the airliner's future was assured when Vickers managed to win a large order from Capital in 1954. The first aircraft was delivered on 16 June 1955 with services on the Washington-Chicago route starting just over a month later. A total of 60 Viscounts were eventually ordered by the company, but the final 15 were never delivered.

V744: 88-90 (N7402-4). **V745D:** 103-139 (N7405-41), 198-217 (N7442-62), 231 (N7465), 285 (N7464), 287 (N7463).

Those not delivered were N7466 to N7477 inclu-

sive plus N7463-5 although these three marks were reallocated to other airframes.

Capital Airlines

When the airline was awarded the Luton-Dublin licence it proposed to employ a BAe 146 on the route, but while awaiting delivery the company leased a Viscount from British Air Ferries in March 1989. The machine spent the next six months or so on the scheduled duties before being returned to its owner in August. During its stay with Capital it carried the latter's titles but retained BAF's livery.

V806: 263 (G-AOYN)

Central African Airways (CAA)

The Governments of Northern Rhodesia, Southern Rhodesia and Nyasaland formed CAA in June 1946 to provide services between the major African cities. A turning point in the airline's history came in April 1953 when a direct service between Salisbury and London was started. In the early days it was something of an endurance test in the unpressurised Vikings, although three overnight stops were made for the passengers to recover. The situation improved considerably in July 1956 because CAA was able to introduce its new Viscounts on to the Johannesburg-Salisbury-London route. When the Federation broke up in 1963, a new CAA was created by Southern Rhodesia, Zambia and Malawi with the Viscounts operating services within Africa. The carrier ceased to exist in December 1967 as a

Above left:
The red and white colours used by Cambrian in the mid to late 1960s was probably the airline's most attractive livery. Illustrated is the oldest Viscount still flying at that time, namely the V701, G-ALWF. *AJW*

Left:
Cambrian received eight V806s from BEA in 1971, including G-AOYP seen on service at Liverpool. *AJW*

result of the sanctions policy against Rhodesia, whereupon the fleet was dispersed to other newly formed airlines in the emerging states. **V748D:** 98-102 (VP-YNA-E). **V754D:** 241 (VP-YTE). **V782D:** 297/8 (VP-WAS/T)

Channel Airways

The expanding Southend-based airline inherited its first Viscount from Tradair when the latter was acquired by Channel in 1962. From this point the fleet steadily grew as the airline acquired other second-hand examples, including a number of V701s from BEA in 1963/64. While some of the aircraft were used for scheduled services and charters, others spent their time away on lease for lengthy periods. Channel was well known for its ability to squeeze the maximum number of seats into cabins and the V700 was no exception. Those employed

on IT work carried 71 passengers, compared with the standard 40-53 with other operators. In 1966 Channel bought the entire fleet of V812s from Continental which enabled the smaller version to be progressively sold. Several of the newcomers were found to be suffering from advanced corrosion so were in service for only a short time, while another two were lost in crashes. In fact, at the time of Channel's collapse in 1972, only three Viscounts remained serviceable.

V701: 5 (G-ALWF), 9 (G-AMOA), 13 (G-AMOC), 17 (G-AMOE), 21 (G-AMOH), 23 (G-AMOJ), 28 (G-AMOO). **V702:** 71 (G-APTA). **V707:** 30 (G-APZB), 34 (G-APZC). **V812:** 357 (G-ATUE), 358 (G-AVIW), 359 (G-AVHK), 360 (G-AVJZ), 361 (G-AVNJ), 362 (G-APPC), 363 (G-AVHE), 364 (G-APPU), 365 (G-ATVR), 366 (G-ATVE), 389 (G-AVJL)

Top:
Central African Airways changed its name to Air Rhodesia in 1968 so the latter was the operator of VP-YND when it had the misfortune to be shot down by a missile in December 1979. *AJW*

Above:
One of Channel's 11 Viscount 812s acquired from Continental, G-ATVR was withdrawn in October 1971 to be donated to the Stansted Fire School. *G. W. Pennick*

Right:
Condor operated Viscount 814s transferred from Lufthansa in the 1960s. On this particular occasion D-ANIP was visiting Rimini. *AJW*

Below right:
Two V806s were transferred from BEA to Cyprus Airways in the mid-1960s, one being G-AOYJ. *AJW*

Below:
The airstairs are just unfolding from the Continental V812 N244V, later G-ATUE with Channel. *G. W. Pennick*

Condor Flugdienst

Lufthansa transferred four Viscounts to its subsidiary for use on IT charters from Germany during the 1960s.

V814: 338 (D-ANUN), 339 (D-ANOL), 341 (D-ANIP), 342 (D-ANUR)

Continental Airlines

Continental became the second US airline to choose the Viscount for its schedules when it ordered 15 in December 1955. They gave good service until replaced in 1966 by jet types, when 11 of the fleet were sold to Channel Airways at Southend.

V812: 353 (N240V), 354 (N243V), 355/6 (N241V/2V), 357-66 (N244-54V)

Cubana

While waiting for delivery of its V818s ordered in 1956, Cubana bought three 700s from Airwork before the aircraft left the line. The type remained in Cuba for a relatively short time before being sold in the early 1960s.

V755D: 91/3 (CU-T603/5). **V818:** 317-20 (CU-T621-4)

Cyprus Airways

In 1965 BEA transferred two V806s to Cyprus Airways to operate the scheduled services between Nicosia, Beirut, Cairo, Tel Aviv, Rhodes, Ankara and Istanbul. Operations were suspended in 1974 at the time of the unrest on the island, but a limited service was restarted during the following year. This time Viscounts were wet-leased from British Midland and Alidair, an arrangement which ended in 1976.

V708: 10 (G-ARBY), 14 (G-ARGR). **V806:** 259/60 (G-AOYJ/K). **V812:** 353 (N501TL). **V813:** 347-9 (G-AZLR-T). **V814:** 342 (G-AZNH), 344 (G-BAPG)

Dan-Air Services

Several Viscounts were leased from Alidair during the 1970s, principally for operations from Lydd. However, the type was also used for scheduled and charter flights between other UK airports and the Channel Islands.

V708: 10 (G-ARBY), 14 (G-ARGR), 36 (G-ARIR). **V804:** 248 (G-CSZB). **V808:** 291 (G-BBDK). **V838:** 446 (G-BCZR). **V839:** 436 (G-BGLC)

For several seasons in the mid-1970s, Dan-Air operated the V708 G-ARIR on lease from Alidair. Most of its work was undertaken at Lydd. *AJW*

Above:
A late production Type 800 (G-BCZR) was acquired by Dan-Air in 1979, operating schedules for the company until sold to Air Zimbabwe in 1981. *C. P. Wright*

Euroair
The airline bought four Viscounts in 1984 for charter services, but in the following year a change of plan resulted in their sale to British Air Ferries.
V802: 168 (G-AOHT), 170 (G-BLNB). **V804:** 248 (G-CSZB). **V806:** 311 (G-BNAA)

Falconair Sweden
Three Viscounts were bought from Philippine Airlines in 1967 for use on inclusive tour and ad hoc charter work. The enterprise lasted for three years before the company went into liquidation on 1 September 1970.
V784D: 227 (SE-CNK), 300 (SE-CNL), 324 (SE-CNM)

Far Eastern Air Transport
The airline began to collect second-hand Viscounts in 1970 for scheduled service work on the routes linking Taipei with various points in Taiwan.
V806: 268 (B-2035). **V812:** 353 (B-2037), 355 (B-2021), 358 (B-2031), 389 (B-2033). **V816:** 433 (B-2025), 434 (B-2027), 439 (B-2029). **V818:** 319 (B-2019). **V832:** 414 (B-2015), 415 (B-2023), 417 (B-2017)

Filair
This Zairean company was formed in 1987 to offer passenger and cargo charters within Africa. Several Viscounts were assembled, the source being some of the carriers no longer operational in the country.
V754D: 243 (9Q-CVF). **V757:** 277 (9Q-CTU), 310 (9Q-CTS)

Fred Olsen
The Norwegian carrier ordered a total of six Viscounts, but it was rare to find any in the company's livery. They were leased to a variety of airlines, including BEA, when the latter was short of capacity in the 1950s, but Fred Olsen had sold the entire fleet by 1963.
V736: 77 (LN-FOF), 78 (LN-FOL). **V779D:** 247 (LN-FOM), 250/1 (LN-FOH/I), 252 (LN-FOK)

Top:
Included in Euroair's Viscount fleet was the 802 G-BLNB, at one time G-AOHV with BEA and BAF.
AJW

Above:
The V802 G-AOHV retained its basic BA livery while on various leases. It was eventually sold to Euroair as G-BLNB, returning to BAF in 1985. *BAF*

One of three ex-Philippine V832s to be bought by Falconair, SE-CNM spent the remainder of its career in Sweden before being broken up in 1971.
AJW

Gambia Air Shuttle

In 1988 a Viscount was leased from Baltic/BAF for use on passenger and cargo services linking Banjul with Bamako, Bissau, Dakar and Sal. Two aircraft were used at different times, but returned when operations were suspended in 1990.
V813: 350 (G-AZNA). **V814:** 338 (G-BAPF)

GB Air

See Gibraltar Airways.

Ghana Airways

Following the delivery of its three Viscounts in 1961, two of the aircraft were then employed on the company's domestic and regional services well into the 1970s. The third specimen was sold to the Royal Aircraft Establishment in 1965.
V838: 371/2 (9G-AAV/W), 446 (9G-AAU)

Gibraltar Airways

For many years the airline leased an aircraft from BEA to maintain its scheduled service between Gibraltar and Tangiers, but in early 1974 a dedicated Viscount was delivered. This remained in service until a landing accident ended its career in November 1988, by which time the company had been renamed GB Air.
V807: 281 (G-BBVH)

Guernsey Airlines

Established as a subsidiary of Alidair in 1977, the airline used several Viscounts leased from the parent company. These were kept busy on either scheduled or charter services to and from the Channel Islands, but in 1983 the company was sold to British Air Ferries. The new owner transferred one of its V806s to its new associate and began a period of growth in the scheduled market, particularly on the Guernsey-London route. However, by 1986 all

Above:
**For a short time Hong Kong Airways operated the
V760 VR-HFJ.** *Via M. J. Hooks*

was not well with BAF, so once again Guernsey Airlines changed hands which effectively ended the
Viscount's regular appearances on the island. However, occasionally the type substituted for the usual
aircraft from time to time.
V708: 36 (G-ARIR). **V724:** 52 (G-BDRC). **V735:**
67 (G-BFMW), 69 (G-BFYZ). **V806:** 257
(G-AOYG), 259 (G-BLOA)

Hong Kong Airways
Two V760s were ordered in October 1954, entering
service in a 44-seat configuration in February 1957.
The aircraft were operated with great success on the
routes linking Hong Kong with Tokyo and Seoul,
but after barely two years they were sold following
a reorganisation of the airlines in the area.
V760D: 186/7 (VR-HFI/J)

Hot Air
See Baltic Airlines.

Hunting-Clan
The company became the first British independent
airline to order the Viscount when it opted for three
700s in 1953. At first the trio were employed on
scheduled services or trooping flights to Gibraltar
and Malta, but insufficient work forced a two year
lease to Middle East Airlines. When returned to
Hunting in 1957 they took over the colonial coach
services to Africa, proving highly successful for this
operation. It prompted the airline to acquire three
800s in the late 1950s, by which time the carrier
held contracts to fly a large number of ITs from
both Heathrow and Manchester. In July 1960
Hunting became a part of British United and all
operations were transferred to Gatwick.
V732: 74-6 (G-ANRR-T). **V833:** 424-6
(G-APTB-D)

Icelandair
Two Viscounts originally ordered by Hunting-Clan

Left:
**Icelandair bought TF-ISU from
Hunting-Clan in 1959. The
V759D crashed on approach
to Oslo in April 1963.**
Via M. J. Hooks

Above:
Three Type 810s were operated by Intra from 1977 to 1979, the V814 G-BAPE being one of a pair.
C. P. Wright

were bought by the Icelandic carrier in 1957. Both were introduced to the company's routes that served the UK and Scandinavia, until one crashed on approach to Oslo in 1963. Its partner continued alone until withdrawn in 1970.
V759D: 140 (TF-ISN), 149 (TF-ISU)

Indian Airlines
An order for five Viscounts was placed two years after the company was formed in 1953. After all deliveries had been made in late 1957, the aircraft began flying on routes to Afghanistan, East and West Pakistan, Nepal, Burma and Ceylon. Another five new aircraft joined the airline during the following year to which was added the four-strong Fred Olsen fleet in 1962 plus two machines transferred from the Indian Air Force in 1967. All had been withdrawn by the early 1970s.
V723: 79 (VT-DWI). **V730:** 80 (VT-DWJ). **V768D:** 192 (VT-DIO), 193-6 (VT-DIF-I), 292 (VT-DIX), 293 (VT-DIZ), 294-6 (VT-DJA-C). **V779D:** 247 (VT-DOD), 250 (VT-DOE), 251 (VT-DOH), 252 (VT-DOI).

Inter City Airlines
See Alidair

Intercontinental de Aviacion
See Aeropesca Colombia

Intra Airways
When launched in 1969, the Jersey-based carrier operated a number of DC-3s on scheduled services linking the Channel Islands with the UK and France. At the start of the 1976 summer season, the airline introduced its first two Viscounts which were leased from Alidair. When the aircraft were returned to the lessor, Intra bought three 810 series aircraft from British Midland, all remaining with the airline until the reorganisation of the company in late 1979. At this point the 814s were leased to other carriers before their eventual sale, while the third machine was transferred to Jersey European for a time.
V708: 37 (G-BDIK). **V724:** 52 (G-BDRC). **V814:** 341 (G-BAPE), 344 (G-BAPG). **V815:** 375 (G-AVJB)

Invicta Airways
Two Viscounts joined the company in 1968 to handle the airline's expanding IT business. One found itself in Berlin to operate charters for West German tour operators, but at the end of the year this activity ended. In January 1969, the company was merged with British Midland, which then became responsible for the type in the combined fleet.
V755D: 92/3 (G-AOCB/C)

Iran Airways
After delivery in 1958, Iran Air's Viscounts were employed on routes throughout the Middle East. All three aircraft could be readily converted into a VIP layout when required to transport the Shah. A single V839 was delivered for these duties in 1961, but two years later the aircraft was leased by the national carrier.
V782D: 297-9 (EP-AHA-C). **V839:** 436 (EP-MRS)

Iraqi Airways
Three Viscounts were ordered in July 1953 with deliveries expected in the last three months of 1955. Operations started on 16 April 1956 with one of the new turboprops operating the weekly service

to London via Istanbul and Vienna. A total time of 13hr was allowed for the trip so it was just as well that the aircraft had a first class layout and only 26 passengers. From the same date, frequent services were flown from Baghdad to destinations in the Middle East, while other European cities such as Frankfurt, Rome and Paris were visited on a regular basis.

V735: 67-9 (YI-ACK-M). **V773:** 331 (YI-ACU)

Janus Airways
After using a single Herald on coach/air services from Lydd in 1983, at the end of the year the company bought three Viscount 700s for an expanded 1984 programme including departures from Coventry. Two actually entered service to maintain four flights per day from each airport in the peak season, transporting the hardy travellers to Beauvais or Ostend as a prelude to the coach element of the journey. Loads were surprisingly good, but by October the frequency had dropped to one daily trip. When the programme ended, the two airworthy Viscounts were promptly sold in Zaire while the cannibalised third example (G-BDRC) was transferred to Manston's firedump.

V708: 14 (G-ARGR), 36 (G-ARIR). **V724:** 52 (G-BDRC)

Jersey Air Ferries
This carrier was formally launched as a subsidiary of British Air Ferries on 27 April 1983. A V806 was transferred to the Jersey-based company for use on scheduled and charter flights originating on the

island, but in October there was a change of policy. The aircraft was returned to the parent and JAF quietly disappeared after one short season.

V806: 265 (G-AOYP)

Jersey European Airways
A reorganisation of Intra produced JEA towards the end of 1979, but only one Viscount entered service with the new carrier. It was used on some of the company's schedules, but the traffic generated did not justify the use of such a large capacity type, so at the end of 1980 it was withdrawn and JEA became a Twin Otter/Bandeirante operator.

V815: 375 (G-AVJB)

Jordanian Airways
A pair of Viscounts 754Ds were used in the early 1960s for scheduled services to neighbouring countries in the Middle East. Later in the decade a series of short leases involving three British United aircraft were also taken, although in the meantime the airline had become Alia-Royal Jordanian.

V754D: 240 (JY-ACI), 243 (JY-ACK). **V831:** 402/3 (JY-ADB/A), 426 (JY-ADC)

Kestrel International
Kestrel was formed in 1970 to operate passenger and freight charters from Lydd, but it was not long before the airline moved its possessions to East Midlands. A Viscount was delivered to the airline on 1 March 1972 to replace the DC-3 which was becoming too small for the business in hand. The ex-British Midland machine was kept busy on IT flights and the scheduled services of other carriers short of capacity. The traditionally slack winter months provided little work, so Kestrel ceased operations in November 1972 and the V815 was returned to its former owner.

V815: 375 (G-AVJB)

KLM

The Dutch national carrier followed BEA's lead by ordering nine V800s in June 1955 for use on its European sectors. Deliveries were completed in December 1957 to give excellent service until gradually retired in the mid-1960s as the company's new DC-9s arrived. There was little difficulty in disposing of the aircraft, so as they were released, they were flown to Dublin for Aer Lingus. All nine were on the Irish carrier's strength by the end of 1967.
V803: 172-80 (PH-VIA-I)

Kuwait Airways

Prior to 1958 the airline was known as Kuwait National Airways, but with the new title a wider network of routes was introduced. A number of Viscounts were leased in the late 1950s/early 1960s to maintain the services to adjoining countries, but no Viscounts were owned by the airline.
V702: 71 (G-APTA), 72 (G-APOW), 73 (G-APPX). **V707:** 34 (G-APZC). **V745D:** 225 (9K-ACD). **V754D:** 239 (OD-ACT), 242 (OD-ACW). **V761D:** 190 (G-APZN).

Lao Airlines

Operations began in November 1967 with DC-3s but in 1969 a Viscount took over the international services to Bangkok, Saigon and Hong Kong. It was transferred to Royal Air Lao in 1973.
V806: 396 (XW-TBN)

Below:
The V806 G-AOYO was sold by BAF to the Spanish carrier Lineas Aereas Canarias in 1985. Reregistered EC-DXU, the aircraft was used for inter-island services in the Canaries until withdrawn in the late 1980s. At one point BAF was considering buying it back for spares use, but its seaside environment has taken its toll with extensive corrosion, so it remains in store at Tenerife North. *BAF*

Linea Aeropostal Venezolanas

This well established South American airline was an early customer for the Viscount, as indeed it had been for the Comet. Three V700s were delivered in 1956 enabling the carrier to introduce the aircraft on 24 March. Two second-hand machines were added in the 1960, but all had been withdrawn from service by the 1975; probably hastened by two of the orignal fleet crashing in 1971 followed by a third in 1974.
V701: 24 (YV-C-AMB). **V702:** 81 (YV-C-AMT). **V749:** 94 (YV-C-AMV), 95 (YV-C-AMX), 96 (YV-C-AMZ).

Lineas Aereas Canarias (LAC)

In 1985 LAC bought two V806s from British Air Ferries for use on its inter-island routes. Configured with 81 seats, the pair were operated for several years before being replaced by jets and placed in store at Tenerife.
V806: 262 (EC-DYC), 264 (EC-DXU)

Lineas Aereas de Nicaragua

Two Viscounts were diverted from the order cancelled by Lloyd Aereo Colombiano, but after barely one year both were sold.
V786D: 333/4: (AN-AKP/Q)

Linee Aeree Italiane

See Alitalia

Lloyd Aereo Colombiano (LAC)

The airline began flying scheduled domestic services in 1954 and intended to introduce the Viscount on to these and the Bogota-Miami sector. Three machines were ordered but only one was delivered before the company lost the licence to ply its intended routes. Its sole V786D was therefore sold to TACA in 1958.
V786D: 332 (HK-943)

This V786D spent only a short time with this airline as AN-AKQ, because it was sold into private ownership after a year. *Via M. J. Hooks*

London European's Viscount operations only survived for one year before the V806 G-LOND was withdrawn. *AJW*

London European Airways

Operations began on 25 February 1985 when the airline's single Viscount began work on daily scheduled services between Luton and Amsterdam. At weekends during the summer it was also gainfully employed on charters to the Channel Islands, but in the face of financial losses the company was forced to cease flying after only one year.

V806: 257 (G-LOND)

LOT-Polish Airlines

Although the airline operated mainly Russian equipment, three Viscounts were acquired in 1962 for use on the Western Europe schedules. The source of the trio was British United, but one was soon lost while landing at Warsaw after only one month in service. Another crashed in Belgium in 1965, but in neither case were they replaced. In

1967 the sole survivor was converted to a V807 and sold to New Zealand National Airways. Subsequently it has served a number of operators and is currently G-CSZB with BAF.

V804: 248 (SP-LVC), 249 (SP-LVA), 395 (SP-LVB)

Lufthansa

The German carrier was already a Convair 340/440 operator when it decided to order V800s in May 1956. The first delivery was made in the autumn of 1958 enabling the newcomers to take over the services on the main European trunk routes. In the early 1960s several of the fleet were transferred to Condor Flugdienst for charter work with its subsidiary, a task performed for some years. At the beginning of 1968, Boeing 737s began to reach Lufthansa, the launch customer for the type, so it was only a matter of time before the last of the Viscounts was withdrawn after comparatively short careers.

V814: 338 (D-ANUN), 339 (D-ANOL), 340 (D-ANAD), 341 (D-ANIP), 342 (D-ANUR), 343 (D-ANEF), 344 (D-ANIZ), 368 (D-ANAM), 369 (D-ANAB), 370 (D-ANAC), 447 (D-ANAF).

Luxair

It was intended to acquire three ex-Pakistan Viscounts during the mid-1960s, but in the event only one joined the airline in April 1966. It complemented the three Friendships already in use on the routes linking Luxembourg with the major European cities, but on 22 December 1969, a collision with a snowbank at Findel Airport abruptly ended its future prospects.

V815: 376 (LX-LGC)

MacRobertson Miller Airlines (MMA)

For a short time in 1968 MMA leased a V720 and a pair of V747s from Ansett for use on the domestic routes normally flown by Friendships. However, by the end of the year all had left the company.

V720: 45 (VH-RMQ). **V747:** 97 (VH-RMO), 145 (VH-RMP)

Maitland Drewery Aviation

After a period spent flying IT charters with Vikings Maitland Drewery bought three ex-Air France Viscounts in June 1960. The first entered service in September, to be joined by a second machine a month or so later. While both aircraft flew a number of charters from several different UK and German airports, work was not easy to find. Some relief was gained in May 1961 when two of the V708s were leased to BKS for six months, but the Biggin Hill-based carrier's third Viscount was rarely used during the remainder of the year. When the BKS contract expired in November, Maitland Drewery negotiated the lease of the entire fleet to Silver City, but before the Viscounts could enter service, the airline became a part of British United. The latter then purchased the trio, which marked the end of Maitland Drewery's short involvement in airline operations.

V708: 10 (G-ARBY), 12 (G-ARER), 14 (G-ARGR)

Malayan Airways

When formed in 1947, the airline operated DC-3s on local services within the Federation of Malaya. In 1959 a pair of Viscounts were transferred from Hong Kong Airways, also a BOAC Associated

Company, for use on longer sectors to neighbouring countries. The aircraft remained for four years or so before moving on to Aden Airways.
V760D: 186 (9M-ALY), 187 (9M-AMS)

Malmo Aero
See Skyline Sweden

Mandala Airlines
Mandala was formed in April 1969 to operate domestic services in East and West Indonesia. Several Viscount 800s were bought to take over the network of routes; some operated in association with Seulawah Air Services after 1971.
V806: 260 (PK-RVK), 268 (PK-RVT), 413 (PK-RVM), 418 (PK-RVL). **V812:** 353 (B-2037), 389 (PK-RVW). **V816:** 433 (PK-RVS), 434 (PK-RVU). **V832:** 414 (PK-RVP), 415 (PK-RVN)

Manx Airlines
When Manx was formed in November 1982, British Midland transferred a Viscount to the airline for use on the London-IoM services. The type then remained with the carrier until late 1988, although

Below:
Malayan's V760D 9M-ALY remained with the company for some four years before moving to Aden. *Via M. J. Hooks*

the identity of the aircraft changed from time to time.
V806: 259 (G-BLOA). **V813:** 350 (G-AZNA). **V816:** 435 (G-BFZL)

Maritime Central Airways (MCA)
Services from Prince Edward Island began in 1941 over a modest route network. In the early 1950s Goose Bay and Gander were linked with the Newfoundland capital, St John's, while later in the decade MCA inaugurated a regular run to Frobisher in Baffin Island. At this point a single Viscount was acquired for these longer sectors, but its stay was short. It was not long before Eastern Provincial took over MCA's routes and fleet, but the Viscount was not retained. Consequently it was sold to Aer Lingus to become EI-AMA.
V805: 258 (CF-MCJ)

Merpati Nusantara Airlines
The Indonesian government formed Merpati in 1962 as the second state-owned airline. An extensive network was subsequently built-up, with services linking Jakarta with many parts of Indonesia. A number of Viscounts joined the fleet from 1970, several remaining active with the carrier into the 1990s.
V812: 355 (PK-MVO). **V816:** 434 (PK-MVL). **V818:** 319 (PK-MVK). **V828:** 443 (PK-MVT), 445 (PK-MVG), 448 (PK-MVS), 459 (PK-MVM). **V832:** 417 (PK-MVN)

Above:
After managing to avoid destruction in the Middle East for nearly 10 years, this Viscount (OD-ACW) was the victim of a DC-9 attack on the ground at Honolulu in 1969. *Via M. J. Hooks*

Middle East Airlines (MEA)

Seven Viscounts were ordered in June 1955, but pending delivery three were leased from Hunting-Clan plus one from Fred Olsen. The aircraft were used on services to destinations throughout the Middle and Near East, plus others linking Beirut with a number of European cities. The type was gradually withdrawn in the 1960s until jet types had taken over completely by the end of the decade. Surprisingly, despite being based in Beirut, only one specimen was destroyed by Israeli action.
V732: 74 (OD-ACF), 75 (OD-ACH), 76 (OD-ACG). **V736:** 77 (OD-ACR). **V754D:** 239-42 (OD-ACT-W), 243/4 (OD-ADD/E), 245/6 (OD-ACX/Y).

Misrair

The Egyptian airline placed its first orders for the Viscount in March 1954. Two years later it was able to commence operations with its new airliners on a network of services in the Middle East, North Africa and Europe. One of the fleet was destroyed by RAF bombs while on the ground at Almaza Airport, Cairo, in October 1956; later replaced by two machines bought from Hunting-Clan in 1959. In the following year Misrair changed its name to United Arab Airlines, so the Viscounts carried the new titles until sold in 1965.
V732: 75 (SU-AKY), 76 (SU-AKX). **V739:** 85-7 (SU-AIC-E), 393/4 (SU-AKN/O), 427 (SU-AKW)

MMM Aero Services

Created in 1984, the Zairean airline obtained several Viscounts, including the two elderly specimens from Janus. While one of the latter managed to reach its new home, the smartly painted 9Q-CAH landed at Ostend while en route only to remain parked at the airport until finally broken up in 1988. Meanwhile, the airline had fared little better because it had ceased operations a year earlier.
V708: 14 (9Q-CAN), 36 (9Q-CAH). **V808C:** 421 (9Q-CGM)

New Zealand National Airways Corporation (NZNAC)

When NZNAC ordered its initial three Viscounts in November 1955, it became the first and only non-European customer for the 800 series. Since its

Right:
The veteran V708 9Q-CAH stopped at Ostend while on delivery to its Zaire operator only to be scrapped in 1988 after a prolonged stay. *AJW*

Above:
The last Viscount to be delivered to Northeast Airlines, in under five years N6598C had been sold to spend its time with a succession of corporate owners in the US. *R. S. Armstrong via G. W. Pennick*

launch at the end of 1945, the carrier had built up a comprehensive network of domestic routes in addition to serving some of the remote islands in the Pacific. A number of DC-3s formed the mainstay of the fleet at the time, but on 3 February 1958 the first of the Viscounts was introduced on the Auckland-Christchurch-Wellington route. Thereafter the popular type was successfully used on the trunk sectors until finally withdrawn in the mid-1970s.
V807: 248 (ZK-NAI), 281-3 (ZK-BRD-F), 428 (ZK-BWO)

Nora Air Services (NAS)
This German airline was formed as a cargo carrier in late 1970, but before operations started the company decided to add passenger charters to its activities. Equipped with five Viscounts bought from Lufthansa, NAS started flying from its Kassel-Calden airport base in mid-summer, but the enterprise was not destined to survive. In February 1972 the aircraft were sold, but even this income did not prevent the carrier from going into liquidation.
V814: 338 (D-ANUH), 340 (D-ANAD), 341 (D-ANIP), 342 (D-ANUR), 343 (D-ANEF), 344 (D-ANIZ)

Northeast Airlines
See BKS Air Transport.

Northeast Airlines Inc
Northeast became the third US carrier to order the Viscount having observed the significant increase in traffic enjoyed by Capital. When the type was introduced on the sectors linking Boston, New York and Washington, the airline was similarly rewarded by a considerable upsurge in popularity. Sadly, through little fault of its own, the Viscount was not to have a long career with Northeast. In April 1961 Eastern began its unique shuttle which offered a no-reservation service with seats guaranteed. Suddenly the

comfort, speed and reliability of the turboprop machine was forgotten by the travellers presented with the attractive alternative. Northeast's losses began to escalate, so reluctantly the airline negotiated with Vickers for the return of the fleet in 1963.
V798D: 226 (N6599C), 230 (N6595C), 232 (N6590C), 233 (N6591C), 234 (N6592C), 284 (N6594C), 286 (N6593C), 288 (N6596C), 391/2 (N6597C/8C). All of the first eight were built for Capital as V745Ds but not taken up and converted to V798Ds.

Pakistan International Airlines
Five Viscount 810s were ordered in May 1956, of which three were delivered in early 1959. Two of these were lost after only a few months in service, fortunately coinciding with the arrival of the two outstanding machines. No replacements were taken on strength, but the surviving trio were gainfully employed on the carrier's regional routes until the mid-1960s when the Viscounts were found new homes.
V815: 335-7 (AP-AJC-E), 375/6 (AP-AJF/G)

Philippine Airlines
When the airline's Viscounts entered service in 1957, they were introduced on to the Hong Kong route and trunk domestic sectors previously flown by DC-3s and Convair 340s. The type had been withdrawn by 1967, when the three V784s were sold to Falconair Sweden.
V745D: 118 (PI-C773). **V784D:** 227 (PI-C772), 300 (PI-C770), 324 (PI-C771)

Pluna retained CX-AQN for 24 years before selling the V769D to a private owner in the US.
Via M. J. Hooks

PLUNA (Primeras Lineas Uruguayas de Navegacion Aerea)

The carrier ordered three V769s from Vickers in 1956 for use on its expanding domestic network, but once in service, international routes to Argentina, Brazil and Paraguay were added to the types duties. Subsequently some second-hand V810s were obtained which remained with the company until the 1980s.
V745D: 130 (CX-BHA), 131 (CX-BHB). **V769D:** 321-3 (CX-AQN-P). **V810:** 316 (CX-BIZ). **V827:** 397 (CX-BIY), 400 (CX-BJA)

Polar Airways

Teesside was the base for Polar Airways when it was formed in July 1982. The company intended to provide both passenger and cargo services with the use of Viscount 800s acquired from British Air Ferries. Although work was found, it was insufficient to keep the carrier in business, so the company ceased flying in April 1983.
V802: 168 (G-AOHT), 170 (G-AOHV). **V806:** 257 (G-AOYI)

Polish Airlines

See LOT-Polish Airlines.

Progressive Airways

Ambitious plans were made by the carrier when it was launched at Norwich in November 1970. A number of scheduled service licences were sought and contracts were obtained for IT charters during the coming summer season. It was intended to acquire a pair of Viscounts from Aer Lingus, but although one was painted in the UK company's livery, it never left Dublin. It was probably just as well because in May 1971 Progressive went into receivership and disappeared into history.
V803: 175 (G-AYTW)

SA de Transport Aerien (SATA)

The company was formed in 1966 for charter operations from Cointrin Airport, Geneva. Two Viscounts were leased from Aer Lingus at different times between 1969 and 1972, after which Caravelles became the favoured equipment.
V803: 177 (HB-ILP). **V808:** 291 (HB-ILR)

Scandinavian Airlines System (SAS)

The airline never placed an order for the Viscount, but four were leased from Fred Olsen for periods in 1960 and 1961.
V779D: 247 (LN-FOM), 250 (LN-FOH), 251 (LN-FOI), 252 (LN-FOK)

Scibe Airlift Cargo

Two one-time Aer Lingus V808s were acquired in 1976 for the airline's freight services in Africa.
V808C: 421 (9Q-CBT), 423 (9Q-CBS).

Seulawah Air Services

The airline was formed in 1968 to operate domestic services in East and West Indonesia. It became associated with Mandala Airlines in 1971.
V806: 418 (PK-RVL)

Silver City Airways

Three Viscounts were leased from Maitland Drewery in December 1961 for use on a large network of scheduled services based on Leeds and Newcastle. Although delivered, before the trio could enter service, the airline was absorbed by British United.
V708: 10 (G-ARBY), 12 (G-ARER), 14 G-ARGR)

Skyline Sweden

The carrier was formed in 1971 to operate passenger and cargo charters to points in Europe and North Africa. A number of Viscounts were bought although some were used for spares at Skyline's Malmo base. During the mid-1970s the company also flew services under contract to Linjeflyg, but in 1978 all operations ceased.

V784D: 227 (SE-CNK), 300 (SE-CNL), 324 (SE-CNM). **V814:** 338 (SE-FOY), 340 (SE-FOX). **V838:** 372 (SE-FOZ)

Sociedad Anonima Ecuatoriana de Transportes Aereos (SAETA)

A number of scheduled services were launched in the late 1960s using several second-hand Viscounts. By the end of the 1970s only one aircraft had survived intact, but Caravelles had subsequently become the mainstay anyway.

V745D: 204 (HC-AYZ). **V785D:** 329 (HC-AVP), 377 (HC-ARS). **V798D:** 288 (HC-ART)

Somali Airlines

The airline began to collect Viscounts in 1968 for use on its domestic and international services. The type remained in the fleet until the late 1970s whereupon the remaining two were broken up for spares.

V745D: 114 (6O-SAN). **V785D:** 325 (6O-AAK), 379 (6O-AAJ)

South African Airways

After the war, domestic services were developed slowly in South Africa, but in March 1956 Viscounts were ordered so that some expansion could begin. The types first service was from Johannesburg to Salisbury on 24 November 1958, and by the beginning of the next year the turboprop airliners were employed on all the main domestic routes. Excellent service was given by the Viscounts for over 12 years, the only loss suffered being a second-hand machine bought from Cubana in 1962. After notable careers, the SAA Viscounts were sold in 1972 for a new home with British Midland.

V813: 346-52 (ZS-CDT-CDZ). **V818:** 318 (ZS-CVA)

Southern International

The airline was formed in 1974 to operate cargo charters with Viscounts. This activity was later extended to include passenger work, often flying on behalf of other carriers short of capacity. This all came to an end in September 1981 when the company went into receivership.

V807: 282 (G-CSZA), 248 (G-CSZB). **V808C:** 291 (G-BBDK). **V814:** 341 (G-BAPE)

Starways

Compared with many operators, Starways had a long career spanning the years between 1948 and 1963. In February 1961 the airline took delivery of an ex-Air France Viscount 708 for use on both charter and scheduled services. In addition to flying on the Liverpool-London route, heavy summer IT traffic meant that the machine was employed on lengthy sectors to the Mediterranean at weekends, using the facilities at Gatwick or Bordeaux for refuelling purposes. The V708 remained the only example in the fleet until the end of 1962, when it was joined by a specimen bought from Tradair just before the latter's demise. Although the pair was kept busy during 1963, towards the end of the year an agreement was reached with British Eagle for the latter to take over the routes radiating from Liverpool. Starways subsequently ceased its operations on New Year's Eve and the Viscounts departed elsewhere.

V707: 30 (G-APZB). **V708:** 36 (G-ARIR)

Below:
Southern International operated ITs with its Viscounts, G-CSZB at one point in its life being G-AOXU with Transair. *AJW*

Starways was another operator of the veteran Air France V708 F-BGNS, albeit with the UK registration G-ARIR. *G. W. Pennick*

Tradair

For the first three years or so after the company was formed in 1957, a number of Vikings were employed for IT work from Southend. This proved sufficiently successful to encourage the company to acquire two Viscount 707s from Aer Lingus in February 1960. However, once in service it was found difficult to keep the pair in employment, so one was leased to Kuwait Airways for a time. A contract to operate some of BEA's German schedules was welcome in 1962, but in November one of the Viscounts was sold to Starways at Liverpool. Shortly after this event Tradair was taken over by Channel Airways and the remaining aircraft repainted in the new owner's livery.

V707: 30 (G-APZB), 34 (G-APZC)

Trans-Australia Airlines

The airline's order in 1952 was the first from outside Europe and was responsible for the development of the longer-range variants. TAA used the type on its trunk routes, adding more aircraft to its fleet through the 1950s. After some of the early machines had been retired in the mid-1960s, they found their way back to the UK for Keegan Aviation at Southend. The lengthy journey proved to be their last because after resale they were broken up for spares.

V720: 44-9 (VH-TVA-F), 84 (VH-TVG). **V745D:** 227 (VH-TVO). **V756D:** 146-8 (VH-TVH-J), 181 (VH-TVK), 197 (VH-TVL), 373/4 (VH-TVM/N). **V816:** 433/4 (VH-TVP/Q). **V818:** 318 (VH-TVR)

TransAir

When TransAir acquired Air Canada's Prairie routes in 1963, the airline's scheduled network was extended westward to Regina, Saskatoon and Prince Albert. At the same time one Viscount was leased but it remained the only example to be used.

V724: 40 (CF-TGI)

Transair

The airline became the first private UK company to introduce the Viscount 800 series when the first of two was delivered in September 1957. Although Transair normally operated from Croydon, the latter was too small for the new airliners, so services were flown from Heathrow pending the completion of Gatwick. Trooping and IT charters kept the two aircraft busy in 1958 with a newly-delivered third machine dedicated to a daily trip from London to Paris and Nice on behalf of Air France. During the next year two Viscounts were transferred from Airwork for use on the African coach-class service, but despite continuing success, Transair found itself absorbed into British United Airways in mid-1960.

V736: 77/8 (G-AODG/H). **V804:** 248/9 (G-AOXU/V), 395 (G-APKG)

Trans-Canada Airlines

TCA chose the Montreal-Toronto-Lakehead-Winnipeg route for its first Viscount service on 1 April 1955. This was quickly followed on 4 April by the important Montreal-New York sector, but by the end of the year the turboprops were to be found

Below:
Transair operated Viscounts such as G-AODG from Heathrow in the late 1950s. *AJW*

almost anywhere in Canada. Eventually the airline had more than 50 in service, so that by the beginning of 1958 it was possible to offer 10 daily return flights between New York, Toronto and Montreal. The Viscounts had a long career with TCA (Air Canada after 1964), the survivors being officially retired on 28 April 1974.

V724: 40-3 (CF-TGI-L), 50-60 (CF-TGM-W). **V757:** 142-4 (CF-TGX-Z), 218-24 (CF-THA-G), 269/70 (CF-THH/I), 271-9 (CF-THK-S), 301 (CF-THJ), 302-10 (CF-THT-IB), 383-7 (CF-TIC-G)

Trans Florida Airlines

One Viscount was purchased by the airline in 1977 to undertake general passenger charter work. Apart from a short period at the end of the decade, the machine remained with the carrier until retired in the late 1980s.

V745D: 206 (N7450)

Transportes Aereos Centro Americanos (TACA)

A number of Viscounts passed through the airline's hands from 1958 to 1976 for use on routes to New Orleans and Miami in the US, plus a number of regional services.

V745D: 212 (YS-28C). **V763D:** 82 (YS-09C). **V784D:** 324 (YS-06C). **V786D:** 332 (YS-08C), 333 (YS-11C). **V798D:** 286 (YS-07C)

Transportes Aereos del Cesar (TAC Colombia)

Three ex-Austrian Viscounts were bought in 1971 for use on Colombian domestic routes, with international duties and an additional aircraft added

when the airline adopted the new name Aerovias del Cesar in 1975. The surviving machines were withdrawn in the early 1980s.

V828: 457 (HK-2404). **V837:** 440 (HK-1412), 441 (HK-1267), 442 (HK-1347)

Treffield International

During 1966 Treffield managed to win some IT contracts for the next summer season, although at the time it had no suitable equipment. Negotiations with Channel Airways secured the services of three Viscount 812s, the first joining its new operator in January 1967. For the next few months the machine was only engaged in crew training while the company awaited its operator's certificate. Once this was issued, the speedy delivery of the second machine from Channel enabled commercial operations to finally begin at the end of April. It was not long before the airline was in dispute with its contracted tour operators, particularly those responsible for the Bristol and Cardiff ITs. Matters did not improve, so on 23 June 1967 operations were ceased regardless of the passengers patiently waiting. The two Viscounts were immediately flown back to Southend to rejoin the third machine which conveniently was never delivered to Treffield.

V812: 365 (G-ATVR), 366 (G-ATVE)

Below:
This V763D YS-09C had a life span of barely five months since it crashed in March 1959 after entering service in the previous November.
Via M. J. Hooks

Turk Hava Yollari (Turkish Airlines)

Five Viscount 700 series were delivered to the Turkish national carrier in 1958 for use on its European schedules. This duty continued until 1971 whereupon the surviving three were sold to the Turkish Air Force.

V794D: 246 (TC-SEC), 429 (TC-SEV), 430 (TC-SEL), 431/2 (TC-SES/T)

Union of Burma Airways

Vickers received an order for three V761s from the airline in May 1955, all aircraft being delivered in 1957. Thereafter they were used on UBA's international routes to Calcutta, Chittagong and Bangkok, remaining with the airline until the 1970s.

V761D: 188-90 (XY-ADF-H)

United Airlines

United took over Capital's Viscounts in June 1961 following the biggest merger in US history. Initially only 41 of the remaining Viscounts were to be transferred, but it was found necessary to increase this total by six in the light of experience. Much of the blame for Capital's demise was unfairly placed on the British turboprop, but the type proved the critics wrong by remaining a popular and efficient member of United's fleet for another decade. The aircraft retained the same registrations but of course were repainted in the new owner's livery.

United Arab Airlines

See Misair.

Viacao Aerea Sao Paulo (VASP)

Five Viscounts were ordered in 1957 for use on the airline's considerable domestic network. All were delivered by January 1959, but unfortunately one was lost that year when it collided with a Brazilian Air Force AT-6. A replacement 800 series machine was soon acquired, but the fleet was more than doubled when VASP bought 10 V701s from BEA in the early 1960s. Most of the Viscounts had been withdrawn by 1972, the last to be retired being the Series 800s that still remained intact. The majority of the V701s actually survived their last seven years or so in foreign climes, many being preserved in various museums.

V701: 11 (PP-SRI), 15 (PP-SRJ), 19 (PP-SRM), 22 (PP-SRL), 61 (PP-SRP), 62 (PP-SRN), 64 (PP-SRO), 65 (PP-SRQ), 66 (PP-SRR), 182 (PP-SRS). **V827:** 316 (PP-SRH), 397-402 (PP-SRC-G)

Above:
This machine was the prototype Viscount 810 G-AOYV before Vickers sold it to VASP in 1960.
R. S. Armstrong via G. W. Pennick

Right:
United took over the entire fleet of Viscounts from Capital in 1961. Sold in 1969, it was not long before N7447 was broken up.
J. Wible via G. W. Pennick

Virgin Atlantic Airways
In the mid-1980s Viscounts were leased from British Air Ferries to provide feeder services between Maastricht, Gatwick, Luton and Dublin until 1989. Only 'OYP and 'PEY were fully repainted into Virgin's livery.
V802: 168 (G-AOHT). **V806:** 265 (G-AOYP), 382 (G-APEY). **V814:** 344 (G-BAPG)

West African Air Cargo
Founded in 1977, the airline was licensed to undertake worldwide cargo flights, but particularly between points in West Africa. A Viscount was acquired for this purpose, but the carrier's activities were interrupted in 1978 when the aircraft crashed in Liberia. No further examples were taken on strength.
V814: 342 (9G-ACL)

Winner Airways
Noting that the war in Vietnam could produce some profitable business, Winner Airways was established in 1969 to undertake cargo charters in support of the victor, whoever it was likely to be. Once the demand had ended there was little work for the Tai-

wan company's services, so the Viscount was sold and the company disbanded.
V806: 268 (B-3001)

Zaire Aero Service
This company was set up in 1976 to operate passenger and cargo charters from N'Djili Airport. A number of ex-Air Canada Viscount 700s were obtained which then served into the 1980s when the airline became a subsidiary of Katale Aero Transport.
V757: 303 (9Q-CPD), 304 (9Q-CKB), 305 (9Q-CPJ), 307 (9Q-CKS), 386 (9Q-CPY)

After service with Northeast, this V798D was sold to the Blaw Knox Corporation as N820BK.
J. Sherlock via G. W. Pennick

Above:
Although built as a V745D for Capital, the order was cancelled so the aircraft found itself on lease to various airlines including Aer Lingus and BEA. In 1959 it was converted to a V793D and sold to the Royal Bank of Canada as CF-RBC.
L. Smalley via G. W. Pennick

Zairean Airlines
Several of Zaire Aero Services' Viscounts were taken over by Zairean Airlines when it was founded in 1981. Passenger and cargo charters have since been flown throughout the African continent.
V757: 303 (9Q-CPD), 386 (9Q-CPY)

In addition to the considerable number of airlines that have used the Viscount, the type also found favour with companies requiring an executive machine. Several Series 700s were sold by Vickers for this purpose, but the bulk of the corporate aircraft materialised from the basic second-hand airframes that became plentiful in the 1960s. Once the airline cabin had been completely stripped, the customised luxury interior was installed. There were many variations but all were finished to the same high standard and contained lounges, bedrooms, entertainment systems and a multitude of devices for those able to afford such features. The aircraft was comparatively inexpensive to buy and operate, so the combination proved a particularly attractive proposition for short leases to visiting nobility. Needless to say, almost all of the aircraft were converted and based in the US where there was a proliferation of customers. Most of the Viscounts have now reached the end of their useful lives with the cost of the extension programme making such an exercise uneconomic.

Military Service
Vickers sold a few Viscounts to the world's air forces, but most of those destined for service with the military started off as airliners. Similarly once demobbed, the transports usually found their way back to civilian life.

Chinese Air Force
A Series 700 aircraft was acquired from Pakistan in 1970 for use as a VIP transport. When retired in 1983 it was replaced by a pair of ex-CAAC Series 800s.
V734: 83 (-). **V843:** 453 (50258), 456 (50259)

Empire Test Pilots School (UK)
Two Viscounts were obtained for the use of the Empire Test Pilots School at Farnborough in 1962, both aircraft having previously seen commercial service in the US. Their new careers lasted for 10 years during which time they flew as XR801 and XR802.
V744: 89 (XR801). **V745D:** 198 (XR802)

Forca Aerea Brasilia
The first of Brasil's two Viscounts was originally allocated the registration LN-SUN for Fred Olsen, but the Norwegian carrier did not take delivery. Before the aircraft was delivered in early 1957 as FAB2100, it was converted into a VIP transport by Field Aircraft Services. Later that year the second aircraft (FAB2101) was taken on strength, but the installation of the special interior consumed many months before delivery in October 1958. The Brasilian President had the misfortune to be on board C92-2100 (both machines were given the new prefix) when a heavy landing removed the undercarriage and severely damaged the airframe. Its VIP passenger luckily emerged unscathed, but the fleet of transports was depleted by one speci-

men. The survivor remained in military service throughout its career which ended in 1970.
V742D: 141 (FAB2100/C92-2100). **V789D:** 345 (FAB2101/C92-2101)

Indian Air Force
This air arm became one of the first to order the type in November 1953, whereupon two specimens with VIP interiors were delivered at the end of 1955. The pair served until 1967 when they were bought by Indian Airlines for normal commercial activities.
V723: 79 (IU683). **V730:** 80 (IU684)

Ministry of Supply
Although both Viscount prototypes carried military serials during their test careers, the V630 Dart-powered machine soon reverted to its civilian identity. The twin-Tay variant's registration G-AHRG was cancelled in June 1949 before the machine's first flight and thereafter it always used the identity VX217.
V630: 1 (VX211). **V663:** 2 (VX217)

Ministry of Technology
In the mid-1960s the Ministry bought two second-hand Viscounts for trials work based at Pershore. In 1977 they were transferred to the Ministry of Defence at Bedford where they still remain, although one (XT661) is grounded. Its companion was still employed by the RAE in the early 1990s.
V837: 438 (XT575). **V838:** 371 (XT661)

Pakistan Air Force
Following the example of its neighbour, Pakistan also ordered a Viscount as a transport for VIPs with delivery in March 1956. It remained with the operator until sold to China in 1970.
V734: (J751)

Royal Australian Air Force
Both aircraft employed by the air force were originally earmarked for Trans-Australia Airlines, but were not taken up by the carrier. Oddly enough, the pair pursued separate careers until meeting again for service with the RAAF from 1964 until 1969.
V839: 435 (A6-435), 436 (A6-436)

South African Air Force
Delivered in 1958, the sole Viscount remained with the SAAF into the 1990s, the longest stay with the same operator to be achieved by the type.
V781D: 280 (150/ZS-LPR)

Sultan of Oman Air Force
A collection of Viscounts were operated by this air force in the 1970s, but they had all left the service by 1979 to return to civilian life.
V808: 421 (505), 423 (504). **V814:** 342 (503).
V836: 435 (501), 436 (502).

Turkish Air Force
When the nation's flag carrier retired its remaining three Viscounts in 1971, all were bought by the air force. Two remained in service into the 1990s.
V794D: 246 (246/ETI246), 430 (430/ETI430), 431 (431/ETI431)

At one point there was a distinct possibility that the Viscount would be ordered to replace the Vikings operated by the Queen's Flight, but in the event the HS748 was eventually chosen. Nevertheless, the type was frequently used by the Royal Family for official visits but the aircraft were chartered from the national carrier.

The Guernsey Airlines V806 G-AOYG shows off its classic lines. BAF